P9-DOD-430

Broadway Christian Church Fort Wayn
Aim High An Olympic Decathlete's Insp...
Johnson, Dave

0000   3863

Aim High

Aim High

An Olympic Decathlete's
Inspiring Story

Dave Johnson

with Verne Becker

ZondervanPublishingHouse
Grand Rapids, Michigan

A Division of HarperCollins*Publishers*

Aim High
An Olympic Decathlete's Inspiring Story
Copyright © 1994 by Dave Johnson
All rights reserved

Requests for information should be addressed to:
  Zondervan Publishing House
  Grand Rapids, Michigan 49530

Johnson, Dave, 1963–
      Aim high: an Olympic decathlete's inspiring story/Dave
  Johnson with Verne Becker.
          p. cm.
      ISBN 0–310–46190–1
      1. Johnson, Dave, 1963–.   2. Track and field athletes—United
  States—Biography. 3. Decathlon. I. Becker, Verne. II. Title.
  GV697.J64A3 1994
  796'.092'—dc20
  [B]   94–13716
                                                                          CIP

In the interests of privacy, some names have been changed.

All Scripture quotations, unless otherwise indicated, are taken from
the Holy Bible, New International Version®. NIV.®. Copyright ©
1973, 1978, 1984 by International Bible Society. Used by permission of
Zondervan Publishing House. All rights reserved.

All rights reserved. No part of this publication may be reproduced,
stored in a retrieval system, or transmitted in any form or by any
means—electronic, mechanical, photocopy, recording, or any other—
except for brief quotations in printed reviews, without the prior permission of the publisher.

Printed in the United States of America.

Edited by Rachel Boers
Cover design by Mark Veldheer
Cover photography by Lon Harding

94 95 96 97 98 99 /❖ DH / 10 9   8   7   6   5   4   3 2 1

This edition is printed on acid-free paper and meets the American
National Standards Institute Z39.48 standard.

■ Contents ■

▪ Introduction ▪

What business do I have writing a book?

I'm only thirty-one years old. I'm an amateur athlete. I'm not really famous, except for six months before the 1992 Barcelona Olympics when Reebok ran all those Dan and Dave ads on TV.

True, I've achieved a few things in my athletic life. I've won the U.S. decathlon championship four times and posted the world's top score twice. I've participated in two Olympic Games, and won a bronze medal in Barcelona—the most difficult and moving experience of my life. I'm proud of those accomplishments, but I still haven't reached my ultimate athletic goals—to win the Olympic gold medal and set a new world record. Perhaps then I'd "qualify" to write a book . . . but not necessarily.

So, why do it?

Because I'm an ordinary guy who, with the help of God and many caring friends, has done a few extraordinary things. I was your classic "bad kid" with no sense of direction who got into major trouble during my teen years. I never thought I'd amount to anything. But through playing sports and hanging out with certain people who saw my potential both as an athlete and a person, I was able to find my true purpose, turn my life around, and eventually become one of the best athletes in the world. I am living proof of what can come about through the awesome power of God.

Many young people today find themselves in similar situations. They're struggling to break out of a destructive life, and their parents are pulling out their hair trying to figure out what to do. I think my story can give hope to both kids and their parents. Perhaps kids will realize that they don't have to remain stuck in a dead-end lifestyle, that they truly can make something of their lives if they recognize their God-given gifts and use them in positive, fulfilling ways. And maybe parents will learn to never give up on their kids, no matter how badly they've behaved.

In this book I've done my best to tell that story, to describe the people and events that have caused me to develop into the athlete and person I am today. It's been good to look back and see where I came from. While my life has not been an easy journey, it has certainly been one of learning and growing experiences. I have been blessed with many people along the way who have cared about me and influenced my life in healthy ways, and without whom I would never have gotten this far. My parents, Caroline and Wilbur Johnson, have been the most loving and caring parents I could ever have wanted. My coach, Terry Franson, has been my link to God. I am certain that without his consistent faith in Jesus and his heart to share it with others I could easily have lost my way. I have incredible managers, Bob Mendes and Mike Bone of Pacific Sports Productions, whose friendship as well as financial guidance has been monumental.

Thanks to my wife's parents, Bill and Wende Jordan, and all of the relatives and friends who have cared about me over the years. I also want to thank my friends in the West Side Gang, who unknowingly gave me my first experiences of training for the decathlon. Even though it took some years for me to use that energy in positive ways, much of my athletic ability—and confidence—began with them. My training partners Kevin Reid, Jack Nance, John Eagleton, and Tim Baker have also had a great impact on my life. Thanks to Verne Becker for helping me to write this book. Without him I would still be staring at a blank screen on my computer. Verne also wishes to thank Patricia Higgins, Kate Coster, and Krystyna Konopka for their typing assistance, Peter Calder for his editorial assistance with interview transcripts, and Frank Zarnowski for all his help in verifying scores, statistics, and background information.

The highest earthly inspiration for this book has been my wife, Sheri, and our daughter, Alexandra, now eighteen months old. With my busy schedule of training six to eight hours daily, traveling, competing, and speaking, I'm often not there for them the way I want to be. But they continue to be there for me as my Number One fans. I love them with all of my heart.

In addition to all that I've learned from the people God has brought into my life, it amazes me how much I've learned from the decathlon itself. Each event has provided me with unique insights into dealing with life's challenges and reaching for life's goals. You'll notice in this book that I pause between chapters to talk briefly about some of these insights, event by event. And I'm finding there is still much more to learn. I'm still studying hard at "Decathlon University," and I'm planning to graduate with high honors at the 1996 Olympic Games in Atlanta.

As an athlete and a human being, I want everything I do or achieve to be for God's honor and glory. I want to be able to say the same words the Apostle Paul wrote nearly two thousand years ago: "I have fought the good fight, I have finished the race. I have kept the faith" (2 Timothy 4:7).

"I can do all things through Christ who strengthens me."

—Philippians 4:13 (NKJV)

chapter one

SEOUL SEARCHING

I CAN'T LOOK.

We are pole vaulting at the 1988 Olympic Games in Seoul, Korea. Daley Thompson, two-time gold medalist and decathlon world record holder, lies stunned in the vaulting pit. On his first attempt at 15'5", his old pole snapped into three pieces with a thwack, sending him flailing through the air and—thankfully—onto the pads. The crowded stadium falls silent as Daley crawls out, dazed. I think for sure he's hurt himself badly. But other than collecting a few splinters and aggravating an earlier groin injury, he appears to be OK. I breathe a sigh of relief for him. Like a true world-class athlete, he picks up another pole and on his next jump clears the bar easily.

In a way, Daley's vaulting experience epitomizes his entire performance here at the '88 Olympics. Unlike the '80 and '84 games, where he dominated the decathlon, this year he has had to struggle through most of the two-day event just to stay in the running for a medal. The world's greatest decathlete is fading, and a new crop of younger competitors, including me, have arrived on the scene. As we stand near the vaulting area watching and warming up, we all know the time has come for a changing of the guard. Who will be the new leader, the new gold medalist?

■ ■ ■

There's really no other sport in the world like the decathlon, which comes from the Greek word for "ten contests." Decathletes must excel in not one, but ten different track and field events over two days. On the first day we tackle the 100-meter dash, the long jump, the shot put, the high jump, and the 400 meters; and on the second day we do the 110-meter hurdles, the discus, the pole vault, the javelin, and the 1500 meters. Success in the decathlon requires a lot of things—speed, strength, flexibility, technique, endurance, and more—but it especially requires the ability to focus.

That's the one thing I don't have enough of right now in Seoul.

From the moment I arrived I have been distracted and overwhelmed by all that is going on around me. Of course, there is plenty to be distracted by: It's by far the largest Olympics ever, with nearly 9600 athletes competing from 160 countries. Entering the stadium for the opening ceremonies, my senses had gone wild. Everything sent goosebumps running down my arms—the music, the colors, the TV cameras, the march around the track with the world's best athletes, and especially the sold-out, screaming crowd, all of whom had come to watch me compete, or so I thought.

Since I had a few days before the decathlon started, I had gone down on the track to watch some of the individual events, hoping to pick up pointers from other athletes. I stood just a few yards away as Ben Johnson beat Carl Lewis in the 100 meters, only to be stripped of his gold medal after testing positive for steroids. I congratulated Florence Griffith-Joyner and Jackie Joyner-Kersee on their incredible performances. And I studied Roger Kingdom's brilliant win in the 110-meter hurdles. But mostly what I did each time I stepped on that track was check out the crowd, marvel at all the people and say to myself, "Man—this is the Olympic Games! This is great—I made it to the Olympic Games!" And the more I talked to myself that way, the more I forgot the task I came to accomplish—to win at the Olympic Games, or at least to do my very best.

In other words, I lost my focus.

I hadn't even prayed before starting the 100 meters at 9 a.m. today, the first day of competition. The news had just broken about Ben Johnson, and a gloomy feeling of "oh, no, who's gonna be next?" is still hanging in the air. It has really cast a shadow over the Olympic Games. It makes me feel that the world is getting the wrong picture of the Games—as if most of us are cheaters. I resolved long ago never to take enhancing drugs, but all the attention the issue is getting distracts me.

What's more, weird things begin to happen on the track. The tension before the first event runs extremely high because everyone is so eager to get started. Trying to get myself pumped, I step into the blocks for the first heat of the 100 meters. My group includes the two other Americans, Gary Kinder and Tim Bright, Pavel Tarnovetskiy of the Soviet Union, former silver medalist Jürgen Hingsen of East Germany, and two others. I am wearing a silly-looking speed suit with a hood, which I thought would give me a better time—if for no other reason than I can't wait to take it off. At the first crack of the gun, Jürgen false-starts. OK, it happens. I walk back and reposition myself. On your marks, get set,—another false start, this time by Pavel. Back to the blocks. Then Jürgen jumps the gun a second time. Three false starts disqualifies you from the event, gives you zero points, and virtually eliminates you from medal contention. I figure he'll be pretty careful now. To my amazement he does it again, and the officials order him out of the race.

Infuriated, Jürgen protests for more than fifteen minutes, storming back and forth and yelling, "I did not false start! I did not false start!" But the judges don't budge, so Jürgen is out. It seems fishy to me, because nobody false starts three times and misses a meet that way, not in the first event, and especially not at the Olympics. It almost seems like he wanted to be disqualified. In the meantime, the rest of us are getting "cold" because we have gotten warmed up and ready to go, and now we're being delayed. Good adrenaline is being wasted, adding to my distraction.

As we step into the blocks one last time, I recall a few days earlier when I saw Carl Lewis and Ben Johnson run the 100. I can't believe how fast they took off from the blocks. So I visualize myself in their shoes, starting as powerfully as they did. To run the 100 meters, you have to become incredibly intense and get your adrenaline flowing so you can bring the most out of your body. Your muscles need to feed upon the adrenaline. The gun fires, and we're off. Pumping my arms and legs, I muster up every bit of energy I've got for this all-out sprint. I try not to look at the runner next to me, but I can feel his presence.

Eleven seconds later (11.15, to be exact) it's over—the first event at least. I don't run very close to my personal best, but I do beat the other Americans. I feel a huge sense of relief that I've finally started this thing. Immediately after the race, however, I have to face the most difficult challenge of the decathlon: relaxing between events. You need to forget what time you ran—good or bad—how many points you scored, or how many people are ahead of you. And you better forget real quickly if you broke a record in an early event, because if you keep thinking, "Gosh, I'm great," you'll waste too much energy congratulating yourself. The same goes for a weak performance: You'll use too much energy berating yourself. So no matter what happens, you have to find a way to completely relax and forget about the previous event. It's extremely difficult. You can't even concentrate on the next event, because that will get you too excited and make your adrenaline flow. Unless you can shut down that adrenaline after each event, and then switch it back on just before the next one, you'll be mentally and physically drained when you get to the later events.

The Olympic stadium in Seoul has a locker room under the bleachers with chairs, beds, and sack lunches where the athletes can rest and wait between events. I usually hang out in there and try to nap or relax. Sometimes I listen to some mellow tunes on my Walkman, or grab a little food. Occasionally I chat with other athletes, but mostly I keep to myself. My coach, Terry Franson, stops in to check on me.

Ironically, between events I *need* distractions to keep me from using up energy. My ideal distraction would be to fly around in a small plane or helicopter and enjoy the view—which of course isn't possible. So I sit back and try to imagine being in a quiet or peaceful place. Often I picture myself relaxing at home, watching TV, or doing the everyday activities that don't cause my adrenaline to flow. But today I can't relax—it's too easy to hear the noise of the stadium.

Before long we're called out for the long jump. It is midmorning, and slightly cool in the shadow of the stadium. The officials divide us up—thirty-seven decathletes in all—into two different groups, and we warm up. Then I must sit and wait my turn. I never know ahead of time when I'm jumping—I might be the fifth jumper or the eighteenth. Officials give each athlete a minute and a half to take his jump, and then they carefully measure the distance, record it, and put the score on the scoreboard. Those things take a lot of time, and it seems like forever before I take my first attempt. In the meantime, I move around to stay warmed up.

Eventually I hear my name called. First I'm "in the hole," meaning there are two jumpers ahead of me. While in the hole, I run around and get my muscles warm, expending some energy but not too much. Then, while "on deck," I run a little bit harder to get my speed up and my blood circulating. Finally, when my turn comes to jump, I usually get very intense, as if I want to kill somebody. I get pumped up until the adrenaline flows, and then burst down the runway. I run faster by imagining that something evil is chasing me, and that it's a matter of life or death whether I can beat it out and get off the toeboard. After I land, my distance and my score are announced, and then I immediately try to forget it—completely—because I know I've got to do the same thing two more times. I'm riding a mental roller coaster—getting my adrenaline up, bringing it down, getting it up again, bringing it down. Today, however, I don't feel enough of the intensity. It's only my second event, and I'm already struggling to stay focused.

I see Daley Thompson standing nearby and decide to say something to him. "Man, I'm really nervous and I'm not doing very well," I tell him. "I just can't concentrate. Could you pray with me?"

"Dave, sorry man, I don't do that," he replies abruptly.

His response catches me by surprise: I thought he prayed like I did, because he was good friends with Innocent Egbunike, a former teammate of mine who was a strong Christian. Now I worry that I've hurt his feelings. I know I need prayer, and I'd jump at the chance to pray with someone down here on the field. Instead, I simply jump. My final distance of about 23'4½" earns me good points. And my ankle, which was sore before the Games, doesn't bother me. But the awkward exchange with Daley distracts me all the more.

After the long jump is over, I have to completely relax again and wait for the shot put to begin. It's early afternoon now, and the event lasts about an hour. I warm up, sit and wait to be called, take my turn at heaving the sixteen-pound shot, then wait for the other thirty-six guys before taking my second throw, and so on. Though it's my least favorite event, I manage a distance of about 47'8", solid but not spectacular. I still feel like I'm practicing rather than doing the real thing.

It's another forty-five minutes of waiting before the high jump begins. During that time, I eat a little bit of fruit and one or two energy bars, but not too much because I don't want to be overweighted before I jump. I also drink some fluids and try to relax. After a while, the waiting time between and during events begins to mess up your mind. You want to be in tune physically, mentally, and technically; but when you're sitting around, it's easy to get bored and even a little tired from the adrenaline that's flowing but not being used. If you aren't able to adjust, it can affect your technical ability.

In a typical decathlon, I have to wait for thirty to forty-five minutes between events. At the Olympic Games, however, additional activities such as moving TV cameras and equipment, not to mention other athletic events taking place, can increase the waiting periods significantly and throw off your rhythm. Doing the decathlon at the Olympics is completely different than anywhere else, even than the World Championships or the Goodwill Games. In those other meets, you may have similar waiting times and even compete against the same people, but during the waiting times, it still feels like a meet. Why? Mainly because comparatively few people attend the meets or watch them on TV. You feel more like you're competing as an individual. The aura of the Olympic Games, on the other hand, is like a magnified Super Bowl, only more so. The stadium is packed at times, and the whole world is watching you on TV. Everywhere you go, reporters, cameras, and admiring fans swarm about. And you realize you're competing not just for yourself, but for your country. Everything is at stake. Nothing compares with the mystique of the Olympic Games. The experience affects your mind and your emotions—and possibly your performance—in a whole new way, and it requires a great deal of maturity to handle the pressure. That's why the older, more seasoned decathletes tend to do better at the Olympic Games.

As I wait for the high jump to begin, I realize I'm not yet one of those seasoned decathletes. Coach Franson stops in to see how I'm doing, let me know my point total, and give me a pep talk. Dave Bakley, another coach who has worked with me, talks to me and cheers me on.

The high jump takes forever because it involves a bar that must be positioned each time. It's a much more technical event, so we're allowed more warmup time and more time to mentally prepare for each jump. And since we're given three attempts at each height, the event can drag on for hours. Sometimes I may have to sit for an hour between jumps. During warmups, I gain the confidence I need to clear a bar, making sure I have my step right. I like to clear a bar once or twice ahead of time so I have a feel for it. That way I'm confident and ready to make my first height. In a way, the lowest height in the bar events can be more important than the highest one, because if I don't clear my first height in three attempts, I get no points for the event; I've "no-heighted." But once I clear my opening height, I'm guaranteed at least that many points and can then focus on earning more. The more experienced decathletes worry less about no-heighting, but it's always in the back of your mind.

Today I open at 6′3″ and clear it on my first attempt. I decide to pass on the next height and then jump again at 6′5″. Decathletes do this a lot—making sure they clear at least one height, then passing to a more challenging one. I feel great after clearing 6′8″, but then miss three times at the next height. Not too many points lost, because my best is 6′10″.

It is now after 6 p.m., and the 400-meter run is about to begin. TV networks usually broadcast the last event of the day live, so we wait for cameras and satellite equipment to be positioned and switched on. Other track and field events are finishing up as well, which adds to the waiting time. The first heat finally takes off at around 6:20. I'm in the second group, which again includes Tim and Gary, the other two Americans. Thankfully, we have no false starts this time. My body performs fairly well—I place second in my heat with an OK time of 49.15—but my head still isn't in the race. It feels more like training. But at least I've made it through the first day, which for me is the harder of the two days. I don't even know what place I'm in overall—probably around twentieth. Right now the top three medal contenders are Christian Schenk of East Germany, Christian Plaziat of France, and Daley Thompson of Britain.

Only slightly relieved after the 400, which ends at around 7:30 p.m., I grab my gear to leave for the day. I've been on the track for more than twelve hours. Outside the stadium, my wife, Sheri, her parents and my parents are waiting, along with one of my cousins, Jim, and Coaches Franson and Bakley. We all exchange hugs and chat briefly. It's great to see them and to know they're rooting for me. But I won't be able to spend any time with them tonight; I still have to ice down before bed. After a few minutes, Coach Franson plays the diplomat and says, "Dave, time to go, you've got to get up early tomorrow morning."

I give Sheri a hug. "I love you, thanks for coming, I'll see you tomorrow," I say. All the while, the day's events are still replaying through my brain.

■ ■ ■

The physical and mental challenge of the decathlon continues between days. You have to settle both your body and mind down and prepare for the next day. My whole body's been working hard, but my legs have been working the hardest, so I go to the first aid room and sit in an ice bath for a few minutes until my muscles get completely cold. Then I get out and freeze while they warm back up. The process serves to flush the lactic acid from the muscles and reduce some of the stiffness the next day. By the time I get back to my room it's 10:30 or so, and I know I need to relax and get some sleep. Tomorrow's first event, the 110-meter hurdles, starts at 9 a.m., and I'm required to check in at least two hours ahead of time, so if I want to eat a little breakfast, gather all my gear, and make it to the stadium, I'll need to get up by five or six at the latest.

If any muscle has worked harder than your legs, it's your brain. In order to prepare yourself mentally for Day Two, you have to completely forget about Day One. You have to act like the meet hasn't begun yet and that tomorrow's the first day. You hope you can go back to your room and fall asleep right away. No such luck for me, and probably for most of the other athletes. I'm too wired to sleep.

The noise level in the athletes' village certainly doesn't help. Thousands of young athletes and their coaches from every imaginable country have been staying here for the past few weeks. Since the track and field competition is one of the last events on the Olympic schedule, and the decathlon is one of the last track and field events, most of the other athletes have already finished, and they've been partying every night, long into the night. The noise echoes throughout the village. I've already had trouble sleeping during the nights before the decathlon, and now it seems even worse. Finally, I put on some headphones and listen to a relaxation tape with sounds of the ocean surf.

Even as I begin to tune out the noise outside my room, I still have to deal with the noise inside my head. I try to calm myself, but all this energy keeps racing through me. I feel so intense, so eager to prove myself to the world, that it's tough to let myself rest. I haven't let go of today's performance yet; I keep replaying each event and regretting the points I'd missed. Then I start worrying about tomorrow and all the catching up I'll have to do. I'm not seasoned enough at this point to put those thoughts out of my head. I know I can do better, and I still feel within striking distance of a medal. With all those worries coursing through my mind, it is probably two or three in the morning before I "think" myself to sleep with my headphones on.

■ ■ ■

Only a few hours later I fall out of bed. My body is stiff and sore. In spite of the ice bath, my legs feel like they've been hit with baseball bats, pretty normal for a decathlete on the morning of his second day. I notice that my ankle has swelled slightly and feels tender, like it did at the Olympic Trials. There, it felt fine once I ran on it a bit and warmed it up. But today I think, *Oh gosh, what if it doesn't warm up this time?* Worrying that something's wrong, I take a couple of aspirin to knock off the ankle pain and ease the overall soreness.

I look for other decathletes in the huge dining area, which easily accommodates thousands. How can so many people be up so early? To one side I notice the decathletes from the USSR, who don't look tired at all. I grab a cup of coffee with my breakfast to give my body a little jump-start. Caffeine is legal as long as you don't take huge concentrated doses such as caffeine pills. Coach Franson, who has a special pass to the dining area, joins me. As I leave with him for the shuttle, I stop in the bathroom and glance into the mirror. At least I don't look as bad as I feel.

You have to be careful which shuttle you take, or you may end up at the boxing stadium instead of the Olympic Stadium. We get off at the fully equipped warmup area outside the stadium, check in, and then I take an extra long period of stretching and loosening up.

The first event of Day Two is the 110-meter high hurdles, a speed and flexibility event. It's one of the most difficult, most technical events of the decathlon, and the hardest to do when your body's sore and tight. At the Olympic Games, the hurdle race is especially hard for a decathlete because of the long hours the first day of getting up, warming up, sitting down, then pacing around. You can't just sit or lie down while you're waiting between events. You have to get up and do a little jog now and then to keep your muscles warm. So for twelve hours that first day you're always moving, and your legs are always doing something. When Day Two rolls around, your body's killing you.

To keep the day's events on schedule, the officials decide to start the hurdles forty minutes early, at 8:20 a.m. The change reduces our warmup time, but I don't mind because, like yesterday, I feel that same anticipation and anxiety about getting started. After stretching and warming up, I watch the first three heats, then line up in my lane for Heat IV. I take a couple of practice starts and try to get my adrenaline to kick in. At the gun, I explode from the blocks, take eight strides before extending my right leg and then raising the left to clear the first hurdle. Three steps between each of ten hurdles, and it's over. Tim Bright beats me with a 14.39 to my 14.66, but I'm basically satisfied with my performance. And, again, I'm relieved to have finally started the second day of the decathlon.

The discus begins shortly, at about 9:15, and I'm in the first group. Waiting for my turn, I sit around, stretching and trying to wake up my body. I've had so little sleep over the past five days that I'm struggling to energize myself and focus on this event. My emotions, my motor skills, and my senses are beginning to feel like burnt-out spark plugs. I can't muster the excitement I need, and, as a result, I don't do very well. Though my practice shots went pretty far, I foul twice in the actual competition before throwing a weak distance of around 139 feet, ten feet short of my best.

For some reason the officials don't bring us out for the pole vault until more than an hour after the discus has finished. Then, after calling us out late, they proceed to give thirty-four vaulters only twenty minutes total to warm up. This ticks off all the decathletes, including me. The officials have been sticklers about time throughout the track and field events, but only to suit their own purposes rather than the athletes'. Again and again they have cut short our warmup time. In some cases it hasn't mattered all that much, but in the pole vault—the most technical of the ten events—adequate warmup is essential so that all of us can practice going over the bar until we feel confident. Otherwise something may go wrong, possibly resulting in serious injury.

Some of us manage to get one practice vault, but we rush so that the others can get a chance. Not everyone does, which only increases our frustration. When the officials put out a cone that indicates "No more jumping"—in other words, it's time to start the event—the first jumper merely sits down in protest. The officials stand firm, however, and when his allotted time of two minutes expires, they call it a foul and announce the next jumper's name. At that, the rest of us also sit down. We unanimously decide not to move until the officials give us enough warmup time. By now the crowd has joined in, screaming and hooting in disapproval, and some of the athletes and officials exchange heated words. After fifteen minutes, an English-speaking official comes down on the field, and we explain the problem. Eventually he convinces the Korean officials to give us all the time we need. The vaulting competition doesn't start until the last guy says, "OK, I'm ready." By now it's mid-afternoon.

Because the pole vault is so technical, it requires more mental energy than any other event. You have to run, properly plant the fiberglass pole, launch your body into the air with it, and follow through correctly in order to clear the bar and land safely. If you do something wrong, you might miss the box with your pole and slam into the pads, miss the pit completely once you're airborne, or even break the pole, as Daley Thompson does today.

When my turn comes to vault, I grab my pole and get into position. Immediately, I am distracted by TV cameras and the huge video scoreboard in the stadium, which looms to my right as I face the bar. As I stand at the top of the runway and raise my pole, I see a camera zoom right into my eyes, and, above and beyond the camera, the giant screen with my giant face. As I run toward the bar, the camera and my video image follow along, creating a feeling of disorientation in my peripheral vision. It almost causes me to stop my approach and start over a couple of times.

The crowd can also be a distraction factor, especially in events such as this that require so much concentration. For one thing, other track events may be going on, and some of the people will be watching those events instead of yours. They may erupt into cheering for someone else at the very moment you're about to jump or throw. Unfortunately, the officials don't take this into consideration. You still must take your turn within your time limit, regardless of what the crowd is doing.

Then, of course, others in the crowd will be watching you, but they don't want you to win because they're rooting for their country's decathlete. They may jeer and make loud noises like they do for foul shooters at basketball games. I might be running for a pole vault and suddenly hear a screech from the crowd. So I have to mentally plan ahead and expect something like that to happen, and then completely focus on what I'm doing. Today I jump pretty well in spite of fatigue, soreness, and my ongoing efforts to stay focused. I max out at just over sixteen feet. My teammate Tim Bright, however, steals the show by jumping 18'8¼"—a world decathlon record. His score propels him into fifth place, within striking distance of a medal. I am so impressed by his performance that I don't care that he has passed me in points.

Besides the intrusive TV cameras and the unpredictable crowd, the sheer amount of time it takes to complete the pole vault wears you down—especially the waiting between jumps. Today this one event lasts five and a half hours, with 286 attempts altogether. It takes so long, in fact, that the officials allow those who have already been eliminated from the pole vault to begin the javelin.

Darkness is setting in, and the crowd thins considerably. You almost need the stamina of a decathlete just to watch an entire decathlon. But the quieting stadium improves my concentration as I step up for my favorite and best event, the javelin. I've loved throwing things ever since I nailed cars with apples as a kid. And there are few things as beautiful as a well-thrown javelin floating in the air.

Warming up, I notice Daley Thompson working on his javelin technique. He seems dissatisfied with his present throwing distance and in search of a different approach. Since I'm pretty solid in this event, I casually offer him a few suggestions. Apparently I didn't hurt his feelings earlier when I asked him to pray, because now he thanks me and even takes my advice.

That's another distinctive of the decathlon: It's common for decathletes to talk to each other between events and even coach each other from time to time. You don't do it too much, because you need to focus on your own mind and body, but you also know that you and the other decathletes are all in the same boat. When you're thrown together with thirty-some other guys for two days, twelve hours a day, it's hard not to get to know each other. There's a sense of camaraderie in knowing that very few athletes in the world have the courage or the ability to do what you're doing. And you've most likely competed against many of the athletes several times already, so you may know a little about them. Of course, you ultimately want to beat the other guys, but the best way to beat them is to beat yourself in each event. You don't really battle each other head-on like a split end and a cornerback in football; instead, you're all striving individually to improve on your best performance. As a result, the competition becomes a bit more friendly. Occasionally between events I'll ask one of the guys (if he speaks English) to tell me about his family or his country. I like getting to know him a little bit, and the conversation can serve as a helpful distraction during the long waits.

Today in the javelin I place second in my group and fifth overall with a distance of 218'. My score moves me into the top ten—too far from a medal, but not bad for my first Olympic Games, I tell myself. Daley has his best throw ever—a personal record (PR) of just over 210 feet, which keeps him in contention for a medal.

At around 9:30 p.m., we gather under the lights for the event we've all been dreading from the very start—the 1500-meter run. It's the hardest one to prepare for mentally. Why? Because you have so much trouble getting excited about it. While you still have a little physical energy left, your emotional energy seems completely spent. You wish that the final event would only require a quick burst of energy, like the discus or shot put. That you could handle. Instead, however, you are facing the longest event of the decathlon—the one that requires the most endurance and causes the most pain. It requires virtually no technique—only guts. There is simply no way your dulled senses and drained emotions can get fired up about it.

And yet, as my group takes off at the gun, I muster the will to hang on for the next four-and-a-half minutes and keep a steady pace. I lock a couple of phrases from pop songs into my head: "I've been waiting for this moment for all my life." "Behind you a runner is born, Don't look back you'll be there." The songs not only drive me forward, but also distract me from the physical pain and the mental anxiety over wanting to perform well and score lots of points. Each lap around the track hurts more than the previous one as the oxygen is depleted from my body. The third lap is the worst, and the hardest one to stay on pace, but once I reach the last 300 meters I release the last burst of energy I've been saving and push over the finish line in 4:29.62. I've made it. My final score of 8180 points gives me ninth place. Christian Schenk and Torsten Voss of East

Germany win the gold and silver medals, and Dave Steen of Canada edges out Britain's Daley Thompson for the bronze.

After I finish, Sheri, all my family members, and my coaches come down on the track and smother me with congratulatory hugs and kisses. I'm deeply grateful for their support, and keenly aware that they share in my achievement. I no longer care that my body's hurting: I have just completed my first Olympics and placed in the top ten, and I feel exhilarated.

As I smile for pictures, however, I hold back a little, as if to say, "Just wait until the next Olympic Games." It is gratifying to reach one of my life goals, but I still have others I'm aiming for: to be the best decathlete in the world, and to win an Olympic gold medal. I've learned a lot about myself and the Olympic aura in these two days. I understand now how hard it can be to focus while the whole world is watching, and how easily I can be distracted. But I'm also fired up about the next four years. Christian Schenk's winning score was 8488, only 300 points more than mine. Since I haven't come anywhere close to reaching my potential, I know I'm capable of becoming the world's leading decathlete. I can't wait to get back home and train, physically and mentally. Number one score. Number one in the world. The gold medal. That's what I'm setting my sights for.

Something else is happening, too, as I savor my accomplishment here on the track with family and friends. I sense that another photo of me is being taken, from an angle high above the stadium—one that shows the bigger picture of my life's purpose. It's like a Polaroid snapshot that slowly develops before your eyes: you can't see the image at first, but gradually the total picture emerges. I know that years may pass before I see today's photo fully developed, just as it took years for me to catch a glimpse of others taken throughout my life. But together these photos point to a God who alone knows his plans for me, who has loved me, cared for me, and protected me from my earliest days. Without him I would not be the person, or the decathlete, I am today.

100-meter dash

PR: 10.77

Life is short. So is the 100 meters. All decathletes feel anxiety before the start of the 100, anxiety that doesn't have as much to do with the one event as with the nine other events that will follow it over the next thirty-six hours. Even the rest between events won't really amount to rest. And the night between is just as much a part of the competition as any one of the events.

Some of the competitors even get sick from nervousness before the 100. I've never actually thrown up, but I've definitely felt queasy. I'm not sure what causes it—fear, adrenaline, or a combination of both—but I do know the feeling is real. What lies ahead is an awesome challenge.

The 100 isn't as technical as most of the other events; basically, you get into position and try to get a great start. In training you can practice the start, but after that, there's not much to running the 100 except straight-ahead, raw energy and power. Of course, you can train for speed, but I believe each person is built with his or her personal maximum. Some have more, some have less. My job in the 100 is to get out there and run as fast as God has gifted me to be able to run.

Crouching in the starting blocks, I often think of Eric Liddel in *Chariots of Fire*, who said, "Dear Lord, make my legs like springs." I try to flood my head with thoughts and images that will make my body move faster—a rocket, an Indy 500 dragster, or even a picture of myself being chased by someone who wants to kill me.

Firing a gun seems especially appropriate for this event, since the runner needs to explode from the blocks like a bullet. All your power must be channeled in one direction—forward. To do your best you've got to attack with all you've got. Once the gun fires, you've got to be completely, totally focused on giving a one-hundred-percent effort. You are instantly consumed with the pounding of your feet and the pumping of your arms. There's not much finesse involved. It's happens so fast—like a blur—that there's really no room, or time, to make up for a mistake and still do well. In fact, if you try to think while you're running your performance may suffer.

There are times in life, too, when you have to dive in head first, cut through a mass of red tape, make the first move, or take the initiative in tackling a big challenge or solving a problem. You can't sit back and wait to see what happens. You can't beat around the bush. You can think and plan ahead of time, but when the moment arrives, you need to drop everything and go for broke.

If all goes well, you can congratulate yourself and affirm the things you did right. You can allow your success to build confidence for what lies ahead. If it doesn't go so well, you may get mad for a minute or two, but then you regroup, identify what went wrong and decide how you'll change it for next time. In either case, you must quickly forget what just happened and refocus in order to prepare for the next event.

In the 100, as in life, there's no time to be discouraged over what might have been. Just as the 100 only lasts for ten or eleven seconds, we need to remind ourselves that the seemingly insurmountable problems and challenges we face each day are but one small part of the whole picture.

■　■　■

PROPERTY OF
BROADWAY CHRISTIAN CHURCH LIBRARY
910 BROADWAY
FORT WAYNE, IN 46802

chapter two

EARLY TRAINING

"OK, HERE WE GO," I announce. "When I count to three, we'll all throw at the same time." It's Halloween night, 1978, and I'm talking to the other members of the West Side Gang, my group of high-school buddies in Missoula, Montana. We're too old to trick-or-treat, and there's nothing else to do, so we've decided to stir up some trouble in the neighborhood.

"Wait!" Steve says. "I need a better apple to throw." He rummages around under the apple tree that serves as our ammunition supply.

"C'mon, hurry up, Steve—time's a wastin'!" Mike urges.

"Don't worry, Mike," I say. "There's plenty of cars out there for shelling."

"Hey Dave—where you going to run?" Mike asks.

"I think I'll go down to Clark Avenue and then jump the fence into Old Man Shuster's pasture. How about you?"

"I'm going to cut through Miller's yard and take my chances down the alleyway. Rick, are you ready to go?"

"Yep," Rick answers. "I'm gonna go with Dave."

"OK, Rick—just follow me," I tell him. "Steve, did you find a good one yet?"

"Yeah, I got one—I'm set." Frank, Fish, and Jace, three other gang members, also confirm their escape routes.

"OK," I say at last. "When the coast is clear, everyone meet in the field by Crowbar's house." I crane my neck to see if any headlights are visible on Reserve Avenue. Yes, here comes a pair in the distance. The cars travel at thirty-five or forty miles an hour on this stretch of road, so we have to get the timing just right. "Ready, on the count of three: One . . . Two . . . THREE!"

We watch in silence for a few seconds as the apples and the car glide toward our estimated point of impact.

Boom. Thunk. Bang. Wump.

"Yeah! Got him!" we yell.

Screech.

"Look out," I warn, still on top of the situation. "He's turning around . . . here he comes . . . OK, scatter!" We all take off in different directions, laughing as we run. Getting chased is the best part. And as always, we don't get caught.

Replaying scenes like this in my head helped distract me between events in Seoul. It still amazes me how those days provided me with early training for the three major components of the decathlon—throwing, running, and jumping. I developed a great arm from throwing things at cars—apples, rocks, snowballs, eggs, even bottles on occasion. My speed came from bolting away when enraged drivers, or the police, came after me. And I acquired my jumping ability from hurdling ditches and clearing fences as I made my escape. Back then, I barely knew what the Olympics were, and I'd never heard of the decathlon. Mostly I just knew how to get in trouble.

■   ■   ■

I grew up in Missoula, a small working-class city in the western part of Montana. My dad, Wilbur Johnson, was raised on a farm in Werner, North Dakota, the third of only four children. I say "only" because his mother had nineteen brothers and sisters. My mom, Caroline Schmaltz, came from a family of eleven kids in the nearby town of Kildeer. Their towns were so tiny that everyone was either a friend or a relative of everyone else. Dad's high-school graduating class had four people

in it; Mom's had twenty-two. In 1952, they got married twice—
once by a justice of the peace and once in the Catholic church
—and settled in Missoula, where Dad found a job with the
phone company.

I was number four out of five kids. Gary and Cathy came
first, then a three-year gap before Barb came along, and another
two years before Mom got pregnant with me during the summer of 1962. Well, she got pregnant, then miscarried right
away, and then got pregnant again very quickly—or so she
thought. The doctor told her that it was almost impossible to
get pregnant so soon after a miscarriage, and that the child she
was carrying—me—might actually be a twin of the miscarried
baby. Once I was born, he counted up the weeks and determined almost positively that I was a surviving twin.

Mom says I was extremely active, both in and out of the
womb. I think I didn't like being cooped up. My reign of terror
began as soon as I could walk—or rather, run. I was always
running around exploring things, bursting through every open
or unlocked door, climbing every stair, scampering into the
street. Once I decided I wanted to do something, I didn't stop
until I'd done it.

When I was just over two and Mom was in the hospital
after having Lois, Dad and a neighbor had just finished building a fence around the yard to keep me from taking off down
the road. Somehow I found the one opening where the yard
sloped a little and managed to wiggle through. Not long after
that, I simply climbed over. Several times as a toddler I fell
down the stairs to the living room, but it didn't hurt. Then I
realized I could tuck in my head a certain way and simply roll
down. It was actually kind of fun, and I did it on purpose from
time to time. I'm sure Mom and Dad were thrilled.

I lived by the slogan "Play Hard" long before Reebok
thought of it. Everything I played with as a kid I completely
wore out. I went through five tricycles—not the plastic Hot
Wheels type, but the heavy metal trikes with the hard rubber
tires. I'd ride so hard and so often that I wore the rubber right
off. Dad kept the old tricycles in the garage and swapped tires

until they were all completely useless. Fortunately, I'd graduated to two-wheelers by then.

School didn't slow me down, either. Once, in fourth grade, while leaping on the monkey bars during lunch recess, I banged my head on a bar, fell, and landed on my head. The school called Mom and she rushed over. When she arrived, she was alarmed to find me sitting alone and dazed on the front steps. The staff had all gone home for lunch. "What am I doing here? Where are we going? What happened?" I kept asking on the way to the hospital. I honestly had no idea. The doctors said I had a mild concussion, and that I'd be OK in a few days.

I got average grades in school, though my teachers felt I could do better. "He's got great potential," they'd tell my parents. "He hardly studies at all and gets Bs and Cs. He just needs to apply himself more." Later on, my guidance counselors also described me as "not reaching my potential." I wasn't really competitive when it came to grades; I was happy with Bs and Cs. I preferred to save my competitive energies for sports. Every now and then I'd push for a good grade, but only if I happened to be talking with friends about who would get a better grade on a certain test. Then I'd study a little harder to make sure I beat them out. But those times were rare. I wish I'd given more attention to schoolwork because later on, when I got into college and actually wanted to learn, I found it difficult to develop good study habits.

My teachers did say they saw something else in me, however: great determination and spirit. And they advised my parents to nourish that spirit rather than break it. I'm thankful that my parents allowed me that freedom (within reason), because even though it didn't improve my grades, it helped me believe at a subconscious level that I could set goals for myself and reach them.

With two teenagers and three elementary-school kids to keep track of, Mom couldn't have worked an outside job even if she wanted to. Yet she always seemed available to play games with me or drive me to my various sporting events. She worked the concession stand at my Little League ballgames and even kept score for the team one year. She served as den mother for my Cub Scout troop. I always went to her when I got hurt or had a problem.

For all practical purposes, I grew up surrounded by women—my mom and my sisters Barb and Lois. They were great sisters: Barb was two years older and watched out for me, and Lois was two years younger. I harassed and teased them endlessly, especially Lois. We also had a lot of fun playing together. Gary and Cathy were much older and usually did things on their own, so I didn't see them much.

I hardly saw my dad, either—at least before I turned ten— because he worked almost all the time. He operated a log-peeling lathe for Evans Products, a plywood mill in Missoula—often logging in sixteen-hour days, seven days a week. And if that wasn't enough, he also served as treasurer of a local credit union, and in his "spare" time rebuilt cars for people. He saw himself as the provider, and Mom as the child-raiser. I don't remember consciously resenting Dad for being gone so much; I just figured that was the way families worked. And though I couldn't see myself putting in the kind of hours Dad did, I certainly picked up a strong work ethic from him that would help me when I grew older.

I do remember some good times with him, though. During my stint with Cub Scouts, he helped me build a racer for the Pinewood Derby two years in a row; I even took second place one of those years. He also built a great playhouse for us kids in the back yard, which I hung out in all the way through high school. Whenever he could, he'd join Mom at my Little League games. I liked looking over from the pitcher's mound and seeing him in the stands; it made me want to play all the better. He'd cheer me on at some of my bowling champion-ships. And a few times he took me to work with him, gave me a tour of the mill, and showed me the huge machine he oper-ated. I felt proud of what he did, and it helped me a little to know what his long days were like.

But there were times that I hungered to get to know him better and spend more time with him. Like all boys, I needed the influence of adult men—beginning with my father—who would take an interest in me and serve as role models. I always knew my dad loved me, but I wished I could have had more father-son time with him. Over the years, I think his absence fueled in me a growing sense of anger that would erupt during my teenage years.

Some of our favorite times as a family were the vacations we took each summer. Mom and Dad would load up the red Chrysler station wagon—and all five of us kids—and drive twelve hours to my grandparents' farm in North Dakota. Since Lois and I fought incessantly in the car, they'd purposely drive through the night so we'd sleep at least some of the time. I enjoyed those vacations because there was always something to do. For two weeks we'd ride horses, go fishing in the "crick," annoy the farm animals, or take out Grandpa's .22 rifle and have target practice using just about anything—bottles, cans, birds, or turtles. At that time it was still a working farm, so I'd help with chores occasionally, or watch Dad and Grandpa brand cows. Usually some of my cousins came too, so I had lots of people to do things with. Sometimes I'd "terminate" turtles by sticking firecrackers in their shells. Lois would scream in horror and run to tell Mom and Dad.

I was around ten when Dad got promoted to supervisor at the mill. He cut back a little on his hours, and we were able to do more things together. He would take me out on Gary's silver Honda 125 trail bike and show me how to ride. We'd put it on the rack he'd made for his pickup and go up into the mountains, where he'd take me for long treks. Then he'd get off, give me a few pointers, and let me ride by myself. I learned quickly, and hoped I could be a motorcross racer someday. I would thoughtlessly zip away for a half hour or forty-five minutes at a time, forgetting that Dad might be worrying about me. But when I returned, he'd be waiting for me in the same spot. I remember feeling loved and cared for in those moments.

One summer vacation he brought along the bike (which now belonged to me) to North Dakota. Lois, then ten, wanted to ride it, but I refused. She whined and begged until Dad made me let her take it out. I pretended to be happy for her, but just as she climbed on the bike I switched off the fuel tank. She probably rode for a couple of miles before the engine died, and then she had to push the bike all the way home. I greeted her with a big grin.

■ ■ ■

My earliest understanding of God came through my parents and the Catholic church. Our family attended faithfully every Sunday, all five kids sharply dressed for the occasion. Gary and Cathy attended parochial schools until junior high, and the rest of us went to the new public school just down the street from our house. Mom would take Barb, Lois, and I to the Confraternity of Christian Doctrine regularly. I didn't really understand much of the instruction in church or in CCD, but I usually liked going because it was a place to meet friends.

I remember knowing that God created the world, that Jesus was God's Son who died on the cross, and that the Virgin Mary was Jesus' Mom who gave birth to him in a miraculous way. I also knew that the Ten Commandments told me I had to be good. But apart from having to be good, I don't remember grasping the importance of God and Jesus to my life. To me it was just a story. I thought I was the ruler of my world.

Not that I didn't have occasional times of spiritual awareness. During seventh grade, I got to thinking about a kid I knew who was adopted. His parents didn't seem to love or care about him very much, and I started feeling sad for him. What a bummer it would be to live like that every day. It occurred to me that he was going to die someday, and that he might never know what it was like to be loved. For about a week I would lie in bed each night, crying for that kid.

But then another scary thought hit me: Not only would *he* die, but *I* would also die one day. I certainly felt loved in my home, but the idea of dying was haunting, horrifying. What happened to people when they died—did they just cease to exist? After still more nights of falling asleep in my fears and tears, the feeling passed. I didn't talk about the experience with anyone, but I never forgot it.

■ ■ ■

My parents encouraged me from an early age to play sports. They undoubtedly saw the energy twitching through my body and wanted me to put it to good use. Practically any sport I tried, I picked up immediately. At age six I pitched for the Pee Wee League. But I threw so hard that one of the catchers on the team refused to catch for me—my pitches stung his hand too badly. The coach actually tried to get me to slow down because he was afraid I'd throw out my arm.

After Pee Wee came Little League baseball, which I played every year until seventh grade. I became the starting pitcher for the team sponsored by Western Federal Bank. I could hit, too, and with each season my competitive desire grew: I tried harder to be the best pitcher, have the best batting average, or hit the most home runs. But I only pushed myself during the actual games; I didn't think about it much otherwise. I played well, had fun, and made the all-star team each year, but I never really took baseball seriously. I didn't sit home and watch baseball games on TV, dreaming of becoming a professional baseball player someday. To me, baseball was just a game, like Monopoly. You pulled out the board, played for a while, and then put it away.

A similar pattern occurred with bowling, a sport both of my parents enjoyed. Mom bowled in a morning league when I was three or four, and she'd bring me and Lois along because the alley had babysitting. She and Dad would bowl together on Friday nights. When I turned eight, they let me join a kids' bowling league with my friends Rick and Steve. I liked it, and again it came naturally for me. The three of us bowled on the same team for the next seven years, with one new kid each year. We racked up victory after victory, and I got all kinds of trophies. I was the league high bowler, the league president, and the league team captain. As a seventh grader I bowled a 223 game. Our team was so good that we were moved up to the next higher league with kids two or three years older—and we won there, too. But as with baseball, I didn't think much about bowling once I left the alley.

In spite of my "just a game" attitude, baseball and especially bowling had their effect on me. They gave me my first taste of what it was like to be the best. I loved being able to set a goal for myself—albeit a short-term goal—and then reach it. Bowling, in addition, provided my first experience as a leader of a team.

Though baseball and bowling were the only two organized sports I played as a kid, I was always involved in pick-up football and basketball games with friends. I remember high-jumping in the back yard with my oldest sister Cathy, who ran track in high school, and Barb. And we always raced each other everywhere.

I did take up boxing for a few months when I was nine or ten. Some local people organized a kids' program known as the South Side Boxing Club, and I signed up, along with a couple of friends. We had one match each week. I was more of a slugger than a boxer; I didn't really develop much technique. But I really got into it for a while. In fact, I pulverized virtually everyone I fought, and rarely got hit myself.

Then one day I took on a kid who had received a few years of boxing training. He knew how to protect himself, and had some good moves. My usual flail-until-he-fell strategy didn't work against this guy. He dodged my gloves easily, landed a few major pops to my head, and I lost. As soon as the match ended, I immediately went home and put my gloves away. I didn't want anything more to do with boxing. That final match reminded me too much of the times in school when I'd mistakenly gotten into fights with guys who were bigger and older than me. My parents pestered me to stay with it, but I'd made up my mind: my boxing career was over.

Sometime during junior high I lost interest in baseball and bowling—in all organized sports, for that matter—and my behavior took a decidedly negative turn. Several factors, I think, converged to bring about this change. For one thing,

Mom got her first job. She worked afternoons at a local deli-catessen from two to seven, which left us kids home alone after school. Up to this point, she had done her best to keep me in line, even though Dad worked so much he wasn't around to reinforce the limits she set. Now, with Mom away too, I seized the opportunity for adventure.

Another factor was the onset of my adolescence, and all that went with it—the desire for independence from my par-ents, the freedom to do whatever I wanted without having to answer to anyone, the need to develop a sense of my own iden-tity. I didn't have any heroes or role models to help me figure out the kind of person I wanted to be; I had never looked up to anyone. All I knew was that I wanted to be *somebody*. So I ended up turning to my friends to meet these needs.

Without realizing it, when I hung out with my friends I tried to become the very thing I needed for myself: a leader and a motivator, someone they would look up to. Like me, they, too, had loads of raw energy and nowhere to direct it. When I got together with Mike, Rick, Steve, Jace, Frank, and a few others, we'd say to ourselves, "What can we do today other than just sit around?" Missoula wasn't exactly a hotbed of entertainment or cultural attractions. We'd grown tired of the usual games and sports activities. In fact, we were bored out of our minds. We wanted to do something exciting and fulfilling, something that made our hearts race, something that made us feel alive. Before long I discovered I had all kinds of creative ideas. And whenever I suggested them, the other guys would go right along.

Unfortunately, my ideas weren't exactly safe and whole-some. Sometimes we'd try something daring just for the thrill. When it snowed, we'd play "hooky-bob," that is, we'd hang on to the back bumpers of moving cars and slide behind them on the slippery roads. Lois even joined us on occasion. We did all kinds of stunts on our bicycles—jumping over ditches, ramps, even each other. Or we'd experiment with firecrackers. Once, around the Fourth of July, I stuck a firecracker in a partially filled gasoline can in the driveway. Of course it was stupid, but

I wanted to see what would happen. I dashed away just in time to see it blow right into the side of the house with a great *foom*. The explosion really scared me—not to mention the flaming gasoline. Dad came flying out of the house, and with the help of a neighbor hosed down the fire. He grounded me, but I think he was more relieved that I was OK and that I hadn't burned the house down.

Many of our stunts and pranks involved cars: We always tried to get passing cars to stop and chase us. One trick we used was to lie by the side of the road and make it look like we'd been hit by a car. I'd put ketchup all over my face, and then lie with my head up against a telephone pole, pretending to be unconscious. The other guys would hide in the bushes and watch for cops. Inevitably a car would pull over and a Good Samaritan would come running over to me. I'd stay still until he got pretty close, but then suddenly I'd jump up, scare the daylights out of him, and we'd all take off running.

As we got bolder, we'd get cars to stop by throwing rocks or apples or eggs at them. We didn't care that we were damaging property—the rush came partly from hitting the cars, but mostly from getting chased. We ran too fast and hid too well for anyone to catch us, even the cops.

The more stunts we pulled, the more cohesive my little band of friends became. We proudly called ourselves the West Side Gang, and we gathered regularly in the playhouse Dad had built to plot new ways to terrorize the neighborhood. But it wasn't long before our rabble-rousing led to actual law-breaking.

I remember the first time I stole something and got away with it. A couple of my friends and I had gone into McClay's, a corner store near my house. While I was looking at all the candy, I picked up a foot-long stick of bubble gum and played around with it. I noticed I could easily stick it up my sleeve. I intended to buy it, but when I saw my friends leaving the store, I just followed them out, forgetting I still had the gum up my sleeve. Afterwards I realized how easy it was to snitch and not get caught.

Eventually we began to shoplift more regularly, though we almost always limited ourselves to stealing candy. During one heist in a local supermarket, something went wrong. I casually walked through the candy area and stuffed my pockets, then cruised the aisles looking for my friends. The clerks kept looking at me, however, as if they knew I was up to something. So I tried extra hard to act like nothing was going on, which only drew more attention to myself. On this particular day I had no money, so I pretended I was calling for one of my friends to pay.

"Hey, where's the money guy?" I said, just loud enough for the clerks to hear. I figured that would throw them off.

No dice. The manager stopped us at the door and made us all empty out our pockets. I remember thinking, *Oh, no, now we're really in trouble.* But he surprised us by giving a stern warning and letting us go.

So began my life of petty crime with the West Side Gang. As we entered high school, however, our illegal activities began to escalate.

Long jump
PR: 24'11"

The long jump demands a less explosive start than the 100, but a highly explosive, well-timed finish. You want to build up speed slowly on the runway until you're at your maximum controlled pace—to keep your stride and timing right—when you let go with your jump. The goal, of course, is maximum distance.

You can't simply go for broke. You have to control your speed before takeoff so you efficiently divert some of your horizontal force into vertical force. If you're running too fast, you won't get vertical enough—you'll have a flat jump and drop your feet too early, giving you less distance and fewer points. On the other hand, if you run too slow, you won't generate enough horizontal force to carry you very far once you're airborne.

In the moment before takeoff, the first deliberate element of coordination comes into play. While running at top speed, you have to make sure your foot lands and jumps from within the designated toeboard area. Most long jumpers count off their last few steps and sometimes make chalk marks on the runway so they'll hit the board in stride. You've got to divide your attention between the board and your speed. Timing is critical.

There's something else interesting about the long jump. The main obstacle you're trying to overcome is unseen: gravity. It's a different kind of obstacle than a hurdle or a bar. You can't run into it or trip over it; instead, it hinders you, holds you down, keeps you from going as far as you'd like. Because you can't see it, you're tempted to underestimate its effects. This invisible obstacle is not unlike the forces within us—emotional and spiritual—that can hinder our progress in our work and our relationships. Just because we can't see those forces doesn't mean they aren't affecting us. They may require a special strategy if we are to overcome them and reach our maximum potential.

In the long jump, that strategy is balancing. I have to strike a balance between horizontal and vertical thrust. Between speed and coordination. Energy and efficiency. Power and planning. Thinking and not thinking. If I succeed at balancing these factors, I'll end up with a good jump and my longest distance.

A great deal of concentration and awareness is needed for the long jump. It's not a very technical event, but it requires a lot of mental energy. I can't balance the different factors unless I pay strict attention to each one during the ten seconds it takes me to run, take off, and land.

Similarly, balancing can help us get further in life. We all have areas in which we need to restore balance—between work and play, between outside commitments and family time, between horizontal relationships and our vertical relationship to God. The long jump has taught me just how important balancing can be—and the high level of awareness I need to achieve it. It also reminds me that I need to focus not only on the outcome, but also on the steps I'm taking to get there. Those steps are going to help me sail as far as I'm humanly capable of sailing.

■ ■ ■

chapter three

TROUBLE BREWING

DURING TENTH and eleventh grade at Sentinel High School, I again settled for average academic performance, and I didn't play sports. School didn't mean all that much to me. Real life, on the other hand, began as soon as the final bell rang each day, and especially on weekends. I couldn't wait to meet my best friend Mike, and Rick, Steve, Dave, and the other West Side Gang members. Whenever I hung out with these friends, I felt the same competitive urges I had felt in baseball and bowling. But now the competition was over who could come up with the best troublemaking schemes.

We still loved nailing cars and being chased, but now we had discovered a new pastime: drinking. My parents kept alcohol in the house, and they'd sometimes have a few drinks on weekends while playing cards with the neighbors. I had noticed that alcohol loosened them up, and figured it would do the same for me. And of course, anyone in high school who wanted to be cool had to drink. My suspicions were correct: Alcohol seemed to make whatever we did even more fun. It made us feel braver and wilder and closer as friends—even if it did get us into major trouble. But we didn't care. We devoted more and more of our energy to the quest for beer.

Of course, the cheapest and most fun way to get the stuff was to steal it. By now we'd perfected our shoplifting technique; getting caught in the supermarket a few years earlier had been only a minor setback. Sometimes I'd go straight to the beer section of a 7-Eleven, stick a six-pack under my coat, and walk right out. But this approach only worked for small quantities. Since most of the time we wanted a larger supply, we started looking elsewhere.

Beer trucks made excellent targets. We'd stake out a supermarket until the huge truck from the distributor pulled around to the back entrance. Then, while the driver carted a load of cases into the store, we'd sneak up to the truck—which was usually unlocked—and take a case for ourselves. One of us would lift up the sliding door, another would grab the case, and a third guy would stand guard. If we weren't able to walk off immediately with our prize, we'd hide it in the bushes near-by until the truck left. We got caught once, but only received a warning.

When we couldn't get our hands on free beer, we'd steal returnable pop bottles, cash them in, and get someone to buy beer for us with the money. We used the same method as with the beer trucks, until we discovered the nearby Pepsi distributor where the pop bottles came from. We'd show up at night, after the trucks had returned from the day's deliveries. They were all parked outside, and someone from the plant would bring in one truck at a time, unload the empties, and reload it with full bottles. Meanwhile, the other trucks sat outside, unattended. We'd wait for the right moment, then descend on the trucks and haul away as many cases of empties as we could carry. Occasionally we'd find full bottles, and we'd enjoy the double benefit of all the pop we wanted plus beer money from the bottles.

Pulling off these jobs took a lot of planning and hard work. We were too young to drive, so we had to do everything either on foot or on bikes. Little did I know that while I was carrying out illegal and even destructive activities, I was actually developing skills that would help me later when I would begin to channel them in the proper direction. At this point though, I had no sense of direction whatsoever.

Soon we began to break into places in search of alcohol, or money to buy it. It started with houses, mostly in our neighborhood. We'd stake them out, usually after dark, until we felt sure no one was home; then we'd bang on the doors and ring the doorbell just to be sure. I always seemed to be able to find a window to pry open. That was my job. Then, since I didn't like being the first one in, I'd have one of the other guys climb in and open a door for the rest of us. He'd give the house one final check to make sure no one was there, and then we'd all go in.

Inside, we'd look for a liquor cabinet or a pantry where alcohol was stored. If we didn't find any, we'd search for money or anything else that seemed interesting. We didn't really care about valuables such as silver or jewelry; we only wanted things that we could immediately have fun with. Guns, for instance. From one house, we got a pistol that we'd goof off with out in Shuster's pasture. And when we got older and discovered marijuana, we'd occasionally find someone's stash and take that. But alcohol is what we really wanted.

When we found some, we'd open it up right there and drink until the rest of our fear, and good sense, had vanished. One time we congratulated ourselves by smashing the bottles on the floor as if we'd just caught a touchdown pass. Then we tore through the house looking for plunder, emptying drawers, overturning furniture, even flinging record albums all over the place. Another time I picked up a BB gun and plugged a toaster and a few other appliances full of holes.

I wish I knew what was going on in my head as I vandalized those houses. Of course, there was the rush of doing something illegal and not getting caught, combined with the reckless pleasure brought on by alcohol. But I think other things were going on at a deeper level. Maybe I was lashing out because my own life seemed so devoid of purpose. I so desperately wanted to be somebody. When I messed up those houses, I felt as if I had the power to alter someone else's world. For that brief time, I felt like a somebody. It was like shouting, "Hey world! This is Dave! You're going to have to deal with me!" I hadn't yet realized that there were positive rather than negative ways to make a difference. Only destructive behavior seemed fun.

The day after a break-in, I would discover that the good feeling didn't last. The antics that had seemed so fun the night before looked childish and stupid. I'd be afraid of getting caught. And I'd begin to think of the people who lived in the house, and how they must have felt when they saw the damage I'd caused. I actually knew some of the people, and I felt guilty.

We did eventually stop the vandalism, but we continued the break-ins. At one point I even snuck into my next-door neighbor's house—and got caught. Mr. and Mrs. Anglestadt were my parents' best friends, and their daughter, Kim, was Lois's best friend. When we were kids, we'd pick flowers and bring them to Cleta, as we called her, and she'd give us cookies. On this particular evening my parents and the Anglestadts had gone out together, and Lois went to their house to watch TV with Kim. I'd been in their house many times, and knew that they tossed their loose change in an old five-gallon water bottle in their closet. So, after drinking a little to bolster my courage, I climbed through the bedroom window and started to fill my pockets with change from the bottle.

Apparently Kim must have heard me from the other room, because I looked up and saw her standing in the doorway.

"What are you doing in here?" she demanded.

I knew I had to think fast. "Aw, nothin'," I said. "I was just trying to scare you guys." *Yeah, right—with my pockets full of change.*

"Dave, you took my parents' money." *Man—why did she have to be so direct about it?*

"Hey, c'mon, Kim," I said, trying to be conciliatory. "It's no big deal—I was just goofing off. Look, don't tell your parents about it, OK?"

I put all the money back and then left by the front door. *It'll be OK,* I was thinking. *She won't tell anyone.*

She told.

Within a day or two my parents sat me down in the kitchen and laid a major guilt trip on me. Mom did most of the talking.

"How could you *do* such a thing?" she ranted. "These people are our best friends! Cleta gave you cookies when you were little!" Her approach was working—I felt pretty awful about what I'd done. Meanwhile, Dad paced in and out, saying, "What you really need is a good whooping, that's what."

"I just can't believe you did it," Mom kept on. "Why? *Why?*"

"I don't *know* why . . . I don't *know* why I did it," I answered. I was telling the truth. I just did it for the sake of doing it. I didn't think about it, and I didn't think I'd get caught.

"We're *very* disappointed in you," they said at last. "And it goes without saying that you're grounded."

That was fine by me. They could ground me for a month or for six months, and I'd be going out again in a week. By now I had my own room downstairs because my brother, Gary, had moved out. Whenever I wanted to go meet the gang, I'd simply sneak out my window. Mom and Dad didn't really check on me. In fact, they didn't know about most of the crimes I committed until years later. But I'm sure they suspected on many occasions.

When the cops showed up at our door, for instance. A few days earlier the gang and I had broken into another house in the neighborhood. First the cops asked me if I did it, and I immediately said no. Did I know anything about it? Sorry, no. Then they asked my parents if certain items had turned up around the house. They said no, they weren't aware of anything.

After the cops left, my parents just looked at me and shook their heads. They didn't say anything, but I could tell they believed I was guilty. If they had talked at that point, they probably would have said, "We've got cops coming to our house asking about you because you're such a bad kid." Maybe they didn't really feel that way, but that's what *I* thought they were feeling.

I don't think they really knew what to do. And I'm not sure what I'd do if I were in their situation. I'd probably sit down with my kid and try to help him. I might say, "OK, son, now that the cop's gone, can you tell me what's going on? What kinds of things are you doing? I won't tell anybody." I'd try to communicate that he wasn't a bad kid, but rather an OK kid who may have done some bad things. That way I could still be on his side and help him to work on improving his behavior. But of course, that's all theory.

That day after the cops left, my silent response to what I *thought* my parents were saying was, *I don't care what you think of me. I still got away with it.*

Actually, I *did* care what they thought. And I *wasn't* really getting away with it. If my parents wanted to believe the best about me, I certainly wasn't giving them much to go on. Everyone in the neighborhood knew I was a troublemaker, even if they weren't catching me in the act. For instance, I used to throw eggs at the Sandman's house across the street just to irritate them. But I'd do it from my backyard, throwing over the house, so I wouldn't be seen. They'd show up at the front door and complain to my parents, but they never had any positive evidence. In return, I'd get the West Side Gang to conduct a night raid on their garden. We'd pull carrots and eat them, and generally destroy whatever else was growing.

What was the common denominator in all of my troublemaking? Simply this: I didn't want anyone else telling me who I should be or what I should do. I didn't want anyone controlling me. When someone put any kind of restriction on me, I immediately did the opposite. Laws and authority figures by definition set limits, so I sought to defy those limits. Even in sports, I found highly structured games such as basketball or football less and less enjoyable because it seemed that coaches or referees were always telling me what to do.

Control issues also cut short the only two jobs I worked during high school. In contrast to my older brother, who had worked all during high school and then left home at eighteen for a full-time job, I wasn't especially interested in working.

During my sophomore year, after enduring a few not-so-subtle hints from Gary and from my parents, I applied for my first part-time job—loading trucks for the very Pepsi distributor I'd stolen from earlier. But I only lasted three or four months before quitting. I hated being ordered around by the supervisor.

Later I worked at a drive-in theater, handing out speakers for the cars and selling popcorn. It was an easy job, and I got to see lots of free movies. But I couldn't resist the temptation to steal money from the cash register—five dollars here, five dollars there. And I didn't like being told when I had to report to work. After showing up late too many times, I got fired. Neither of my bosses for these two jobs had made unreasonable demands of me; I simply revolted whenever I encountered limits or restrictions.

I think my defiant attitude stemmed in part from my parents, who probably gave me too much freedom and not enough structure as a kid. They taught me high moral standards, and tried to set limits again and again. But they weren't able to enforce those limits effectively with Dad working all the time and Mom chasing after four other kids. As a result, I didn't bump up against enough firm restrictions as a kid to develop a healthy respect for limits as a teenager.

I'm not blaming my parents for my behavior; I know they always loved me and tried to raise me right. I made many bad choices along the way, and I alone must accept responsibility for those choices. But understanding the conditions under which I made those choices has helped me to grow, and I hope it will help me to be a good parent to my kids someday.

■ ■ ■

In spite of occasional close calls with my parents and with the police, I kept searching for new supplies of alcohol.

One evening at around seven, I felt like snooping around the neighborhood. I couldn't find anyone to go along, so I went alone. A few blocks down the street was a pizza place where my parents sometimes brought us kids. As I went in, I noticed a bar next door that looked like it might be connected. Perhaps

I'd be able to sneak through one of the places into the other. I checked the bathroom of the pizza place, and sure enough, found an unlocked door into the bar.

A plan began forming in my head. Later that evening after the pizza place had closed, I went back, walked into the bar, and asked if I could use the bathroom. No problem. When no one was looking, I slipped through the same door I'd found earlier and tiptoed into the empty pizza joint. Then I quietly unlocked (but did not open) the back door leading outside, returned to the bathroom, and walked back out through the bar, so they could see me leave. After the bar closed a few hours later, I returned again and tried the door I'd unlocked. Bingo. It was now around three in the morning, and I had the bar and the pizza joint to myself. Naturally, I went for the alcohol.

As I was walking into the bar, I heard clicking noises and noticed a little red light flashing—possibly a motion-sensing alarm. I ran back to the door I'd entered through and waited by the back of the pizza shop to see if any cops showed up at the bar. If they came, I'd be able to dart away unnoticed. But after fifteen or twenty minutes all was still silent, so I went back in.

First I found a six-foot-tall bottle of wine with a curly neck. That would be fun to show the guys, and even more fun to try and drink from, I thought. So I set it aside. Then I opened the storage area and rolled out a keg of Budweiser. Finally, I selected around a dozen bottles of hard liquor. While poking around in some drawers, I discovered the keys to a Coke machine and a can of police-strength mace. I opened up the pop machine for money, but found only a few quarters, so as "punishment" I sprayed all the cans inside the machine with mace. Then, just for fun, I blasted some of the other bar equipment. As I turned to leave, however, I realized something: How was I going to get all this stuff home? I didn't have a car; in fact, I didn't have my driver's license yet, though I knew how to drive.

Then a thought occurred to me: the pizza place had delivery trucks parked outside. In the kitchen next to the door I saw a row of keys hanging on the wall, numbered to correspond with the trucks. Grabbing a set, I went outside and tried the truck door. Yes. Moments later I had pulled up the truck to the back door and loaded everything into it except the keg, which was too heavy to lift. I rolled it over into the bushes to retrieve shortly. Without even considering who might see me, I drove the truck home, parked it right in front of my house, hid all the loot in the playhouse, then drove back to the restaurant. Carefully, I hung up the key and locked the doors to avoid detection and make it possible for me to do it again sometime.

Last of all, I had to get the 200-pound keg home. Without anyone to help me lift it at four in the morning, there was only one option: I rolled that thing the entire four blocks to my house. The first block or so was dirt, so the barrel rolled quietly, but when I reached the pavement it clanked noisily in the night. I thought for sure the neighbors would hear, but I made it all the way to my house without incident, and hid the keg in back. Success!

I couldn't wait to tell the whole story to my friends. The next night the West Side Gang had quite a party. Since we had no tap, we bashed in the cork and poured right from the keg.

By the end of our sophomore year at Sentinel, most of us had gotten our driver's licenses. Until then, we'd been walking or riding our bikes everywhere. Sometimes we'd steal bikes if we happened to need them, though we never kept or sold them; we always dropped them off somewhere. Once we had cars, however, we left the bikes alone. I didn't have my own car, but my parents sometimes let me drive their 1964 Ford Comet. Since most of us in the gang didn't have jobs, we had to steal gas in order to drive. Sometimes we'd siphon it from another car, or else we'd find places with their own private gas pumps. We'd simply hop the fence and fill up our gas cans. I was amazed that the pumps were never locked.

Now that we had access to wheels, we eagerly joined the school party scene. And we took it upon ourselves to bring beer whenever we could find or steal it. But the demand was high, and our supply was low. What was a beer hunter to do?

Watch for opportunities. One night during the fall of my junior year, I unexpectedly came upon the opportunity of a lifetime—or so I thought. It was after midnight, and, as usual, I wanted to prowl, so I had snuck out my window and was roaming around the neighborhood. I stopped at Mike's and Fish's houses and tapped on their windows to get them out of bed, but to no avail.

Walking back home, I was just about to give up for the night when I noticed a car parked in front of the Sandman's house. It had a red Budweiser logo on the door—some kind of company car. I'd seen it earlier, but hadn't stopped to think it might have beer in it. Deciding to take a quick look, I peered through the side window.

No beer. But I did notice a large ring of keys, perhaps fifteen in all, lying on the seat. The idea occurred to me to start a key collection. I'd keep my eyes open wherever I went, and any time I saw keys I'd take them—just so I could say I did it. At that point it didn't cross my mind to *do* anything with the keys—I just wanted to collect them. And I figured this fat ring would make a good starter set, so I grabbed it.

A few days later, while my friends and I were hanging around in front of my house, a man strolled over from Sandman's place—one of his sons.

"Hey, have you guys seen any keys lying around here?" he casually asked. "I really need them—they go to the place I work, and I think they might have fallen out of my car. If you see them around, could you bring 'em over to me?"

Gee, sorry, we hadn't seen any, but we'd be sure to let him know if we found them.

A little later it hit me: the place he worked was a Budweiser place. And I had the keys. Could I have actually gained access to an unlimited supply of beer?

First we had to find the place. After checking the phone book and driving around, we located a big warehouse on the other side of town. Then, a few nights later, six or seven of us went back, parked our cars down the street, and strode up to the side door. On it was a large "Beware of Dog" sign. We didn't see any dogs, but just to be sure, we banged on the door and the windows and listened for barking. The noise would probably also trigger a sound or vibration alarm if there was one. We sat in the bushes for a while, and when no dogs or cops appeared, we started trying keys in the door. Sure enough, one of them turned both the deadbolt and the knob lock, and the door clicked open. The magic key.

My heart raced with excitement and fear as we proceeded very slowly with our flashlights into a dark hallway. On the right were doors leading into offices, and behind the left wall, we guessed, was the warehouse area. We were still terrified that a guard dog might suddenly attack us; maybe some dog specially trained to kill without barking. And motion sensors could set off an alarm, so that worried us, too. It seemed like a long time before we reached the end of the hall and opened the door into the warehouse.

What an incredible sight.

Aisles and aisles of beer, more than we could drink in a lifetime, stacked to the ceiling. Cases upon cases of every imaginable alcoholic beverage. All ours for the taking.

We hardly knew where to start. The thrill of our discovery quickly dissipated the fear of dogs and alarms, and we began to wander up and down the rows, surveying the supplies and trying to decide what to take. Several lights were apparently left on in the room at all times, enabling us to see without any trouble. Besides the expected Bud and Bud Light, we found other beers, ales, wines, and concoctions we'd never heard of. We sampled all of it. There was also a keg room, so we lugged one out to take with us. We felt like little kids who'd been set loose in Toys R Us.

Unlike many of our previous break-ins, we made sure not to get out of control or break bottles or mess things up; we knew we'd be coming back and didn't want to arouse suspicion. We got a little drunk from all the sampling, however, and slipped up at one point when we found a room full of Budweiser paraphernalia—t-shirts, suspenders, hats, beer can holders, and so on. We tried all the keys, but none of them opened the door, so we kicked it in with our big hiking boots. The damage wasn't too noticeable, though, and we managed to restore it to working condition.

After two hours of drinking and discovery in this newly found paradise, we decided to collect our treasure and take it home. We didn't want to use the same door we entered by because the outside area was too well-lit, so we carried everything to the rear loading dock. We found the control box for the huge garage doors, and raised one of them only a few feet, just high enough for us to slip under. Moving quickly now, we carted everything out underneath the garage door and stacked it in a dark corner. Going back inside, we closed the dock door, retraced our steps and cleaned up, making sure the place looked the way we found it. All the bottles and cans we'd drunk from went into the garbage—not really a smart place, since someone could notice them and get suspicious. (They did get suspicious, I later learned, but only of the employees.) Then we left the building through the original entry door and locked it.

Finally, one of the guys drove the car around to the back, where we loaded it up in about three minutes and then blew out of there as fast as we could.

"Yeah, we did it!" we yelled in the car. "This is *it*—the best we've ever done!" The whole way home we whooped and gave each other high fives. We were so jazzed that we'd pulled such a big heist and gotten away with it. Not to mention dead tired from all the hard "work" we'd done.

But this was only the beginning. The warehouse wasn't a one-time job like the pizza place; I still had the magic key, so we could go back as often as we liked. The potential seemed enormous, and our beer supply unlimited. Incredible.

We returned to the warehouse pretty much every week for the next seven or eight months. I lost track of all the parties we either sponsored or provided alcohol for. Sometimes we'd bring other friends to help us select what we needed for the next week's party, and once or twice we had as many as ten people in the building. It still amazes me that we went for that long without getting caught. We were amateurs, and we did little to escape detection other than cleaning up after ourselves. We never wore gloves or worried about fingerprints, and never cared that our used bottles and cans were left in the garbage. After a while we didn't worry about making noise, either. Probably the smartest thing we did was take limited quantities and a variety of brands so that people wouldn't notice a large amount of stock missing from one place. We dumped the used kegs into drainage pipes around town.

About two months after that first night, we had a major scare. A bunch of us were doing our weekly "shopping," when all of a sudden the ring of an extremely loud bell pierced the air. "Oh no—an alarm!" someone gasped. "What're we gonna do?" Instantly everyone started to panic and scramble for the doors.

"Wait a minute, guys—don't freak out!" I said, taking charge. "Listen!"

The ear-splitting sound of the bell continued as we stood there, hearts pounding. The rhythm seemed familiar—three seconds on, three seconds off, three on, three off. It stopped after about a minute. A moment later I realized what it was.

"I don't think it's an alarm," I said at last, still cautious. "The rhythm's too steady. It's gotta be a telephone." Probably one of those phones with the extra-loud ringer so they could hear it over the warehouse noise.

Just to be sure, however, I told everyone to get down until we felt the coast was clear. Several of us watched the parking lot from a window where we couldn't be seen. Ten minutes ticked by. Then, just as I began to relax, a lone police car came slowly down the street, and turned the corner into the warehouse lot. He definitely seemed to be looking for something. We all froze as the spotlight on his car moved around the edges of the building, then shone right in our direction. Finally, after twenty incredibly long seconds, he turned around and drove off, apparently convinced that all was OK.

We started to get up and leave, but figured we'd be admitting defeat if we left empty-handed, so we quickly collected what we wanted and then took off, feeling shaky but still proud that we'd outsmarted the cops.

If indeed the bell was only a phone, it seemed like too much of a coincidence that the cop showed up. We theorized afterwards that someone had dialed the number on purpose to scare would-be burglars. The cop would then nab the thieves as they fled. But who knows? And if they were really trying to catch a thief, why didn't the cop come in?

We skipped a couple of weeks before going back. But before long, we resumed our normal schedule and kept it up for another four or five months.

As spring came and the school year began to wind down, the West Side Gang planned to supply kegs for a major party at one of Mike's friends' houses. We wanted to go all out and make it a big bash. So on Thursday night we hopped in the car for our usual run to the Bud warehouse. It would turn out to be anything but usual.

When I stuck the key into the door, it wouldn't turn. There must be something wrong with the lock, I thought, and kept trying. I pulled it out and shoved it back in several times, wiggled it like crazy, and finally tried to force it in both directions.

Snap.

My magic key had just lost its magic.

Half of it lay in my hand, and the other half remained in the lock. I stood there in disbelief. They must have changed the locks. What lousy timing! Now what would we do?

We didn't even consider backing out of the party. We simply had to have the kegs of beer. Where else could we find that much? Ripping off a beer truck wouldn't bring in nearly enough. So we went around the building, selected a strategic window to break, unlatched it, and let ourselves in. We spent only fifteen or twenty minutes inside, but still rounded up everything we needed—the kegs, a few extra cases of regular beer, and several bottles of wine. Then we split, disappointed that we'd lost our key access, but relieved that we'd still be able to have the party on Friday.

It was a great party, with lots of girls and lots of beer. The parents had gone away for the weekend and we had the whole house to ourselves. We were a hit because of the excellent variety of alcohol we provided. I bounced around from "tending bar" to dancing with my girlfriend to laughing with the other guys, drinking all the while.

But inside I did not feel good about the situation we'd gotten into. We were having a party with "overtly" stolen kegs. Before, when I had the keys, it seemed more like we were shopping. Now it was breaking and entering, and I knew the incident would be reported to the police.

Saturday morning I woke up feeling hung over and leery about the previous night. Sure enough, the phone rang and it was Mike. The cops had just shown up at his friend's house and confiscated the kegs we'd left behind. Apparently they'd gotten a lead from someone at the party who knew someone at the Bud warehouse. Mike's friend had given the police two names: Mike's and mine.

Panicking over the phone, we first tried to plot out how we'd protect the rest of the group. But after several long conversations with each other and some of the other guys, we decided we'd all confess together. I'd hardly hung up the phone when there came a knock at the door. I knew who it was, so I let my parents answer.

"Mr. and Mrs. Johnson," the policeman said, "we need to have you and your son come down to the station. We want to question him."

Mom and Dad didn't appear alarmed at first; they'd gotten used to police visits at the house. They just wore their usual disappointed looks as we drove to the station. But once they heard about the extent of my criminal activity, they grew much more concerned. I started crying in front of them and the police, offering up any excuse I could think of. I tried to divert the blame, saying that I didn't cause everything, that the others helped, and that I probably wouldn't have done it if my friends weren't along. Of course, the other guys would say the same thing so that none of us would be considered the leader.

So far the police had only questioned us about the most recent break-in; that's all they had evidence for. Then they asked about the keys. I thought about lying and saying that we only went to the warehouse that one time and found a broken key in the door, but I ended up confessing to having the keys all along. We didn't know how much we'd stolen; we could only say that we took a lot. They also asked about other local unsolved mysteries, such as the bar and pizza joint break-in, and the numerous houses that had been burglarized. This time we did lie, and said we knew nothing about those. We limited our confession to the Budweiser racket.

And what a racket it turned out to be. After taking inventory, the owner determined that we had stolen well over five thousand dollars' worth of alcohol. That number seemed awfully high to me, but then again, we'd stocked a lot of parties. Something would have to be done about such a huge theft, we were told.

I was scared. If the owner of the warehouse pressed charges, we could be convicted and sent to a juvenile detention facility. We'd have a criminal record. This was the first time I really had to face the law. I'd laughed at it many times, but not now. Dad didn't know what to do with me: On the one hand, he knew it would probably help me to experience the consequences of my actions; but on the other, he hated to see me in such trouble and wanted to protect me from suffering too much.

After a long conversation between Dad, the owner, and the police, they came up with a "diversion agreement" which required us to work for the owner until the stolen goods were paid off. We'd have to spend the summer sweeping, chopping weeds, and doing other odd jobs at the warehouse. In exchange, the owner wouldn't press charges and nothing would go on our record.

I should have felt an overwhelming debt of gratitude toward the warehouse owner. Instead, I was so relieved at the settlement that I soon got cocky again. We worked pretty hard outside the warehouse, but occasionally when we were near a door we'd still grab a case of beer and hide it in the weeds. We also worked at the owner's house, mowing the lawn and cleaning the garage. It just so happened that his garage was stacked with more cases of alcohol, so we made sure to "borrow" one of those every now and then. Another time he sent us to a beautiful piece of lake property, where our job was to clean and prepare a dance hall for a big party. We ended up staying around and joining in the festivities.

I've never completely understood why I felt so compelled to defy all limits and structures placed on me. Was it the youthful illusion of invincibility? Repressed anger? Misdirected energy? The search for significance? Probably all of the above. But even after getting caught, that raw, uncontrolled energy showed no sign of letting up. We were already devising new ways to steal more alcohol. We wanted to learn where hard liquor was distributed from so we could set up a new operation. And we still didn't hesitate to take advantage of our usual troublemaking opportunities.

One seemingly harmless stunt we pulled nearly landed us in jail. It was early summer, and Mike and I were driving in his dad's truck. Ahead I saw a little kid walking along the road, and I thought it'd be fun to scare him.

"Hey Mike," I said, "Swerve at this kid and I'll open the door and pretend I'm gonna hit him with the door." He swerved, and I swung the door open, yanking it shut just in time. I saw the split-second look of terror on the boy's face, and his desperate lunge. I'm ashamed to even admit that I found pleasure in such an act.

Later on, however, the police showed up at Mike's house, where the truck sat in the driveway. They were looking for two guys who'd hit a little kid. They had to be talking about us, but something seemed fishy to me, since I honestly didn't believe I had hit him. Before we knew it, the cops had formally charged us with aggravated assault.

Suddenly, we found ourselves in a much more serious situation than the Budweiser escapade. This time the district attorney and the kid's parents wanted to prosecute us as adults. They wanted us to pay for our crime. That would mean court appearances, a trial, and possibly jail if we were convicted. But I still insisted that I hadn't hit the boy. What I'd done was cruel and dangerous and wrong, but not a crime. My parents and Mike's parents combined to hire a lawyer, and he went to work on the case.

So the summer of 1980 turned out to be pretty sobering. I had to meet with the lawyer and appear in court a few times, plus I continued working at the Budweiser distributor. All because of trouble I'd gotten myself into. As I looked ahead to my senior year of high school, I began to think that I should do something with that year—something I could call an accomplishment. I hadn't played any sports, but my friends had told me I was fast and that I should go out for football or track, so maybe I'd try a sport and see what I could do. Actually, that previous spring I had dabbled in track: I tried the hurdles, the javelin, and the high jump, but I rarely showed up for practices and only competed in two or three meets. I hardly considered myself a part of the team. Mike played football, though; I might join the team with him when practices began in August. These musings certainly didn't represent any fundamental change in who I was as a person. But perhaps they arose from some small part of me that wanted to take my life in a more positive direction.

Little did I know that I would soon be *forced* to go in another direction—out of state. Dad's company, Evans Products, had decided to shut down its plant in Missoula. Business had been declining for several years, and finally they had no choice but to close their doors. I had sensed for the past few months that Dad wasn't quite himself, but with all the trouble I was getting into I had never asked why. When I heard the news from Mom, I was stunned. Dad would still have a job, but he'd have to relocate to a different plant, either in Raleigh, North Carolina, or Corvallis, Oregon. They were as upset about moving as I was. They, too, liked Missoula and didn't want to leave; besides, Gary and Cathy had settled in the area, and we were only a twelve-hour drive from all our North Dakota relatives. After agonizing over it for several weeks, they decided to choose Corvallis because it was closer to family.

I refused to believe it would happen. What about all my friends? I'd never see them again. And I'd have to go to a strange school in a new city for my senior year. I kept telling myself, *Don't worry—things will change at the plant, business will pick up again, and we'll all be able to stay right here.* But nothing changed, and the horrible reality of moving away began to sink in.

Meanwhile, I still had legal problems to clear up. The lawyer had carefully researched the incident with the little boy and concluded that virtually all the evidence was circumstantial. To my great relief (and my parents'), he convinced the court to drop the case. He had also looked into the Budweiser affair and found enough discrepancies that it was dropped too, and we didn't have to continue working there.

My brushes with the law had their effect on me, however. I began to give myself the same labels that others were using about me: Troublemaker. Bad Kid. The guy who'd never amount to anything. I was having fun much of the time, but my "fun" all too often occurred at the expense of other people or their property. If I didn't make some changes in my life soon, I realized, I'd be headed for an extended stay in prison. The problem was, I didn't know how to change. I didn't really think it was possible to change. So I just figured I was stuck being a bad kid, and if that's who I was, there was nothing I could do.

My friends and I tried to enjoy our last few weeks together. I felt sad to leave them, and afraid to be on my own without them. I had depended on them for fun and camaraderie, but even more so for my sense of identity and self-worth. Because they looked up to me, and I to them, I felt OK about myself. Now I'd have to discover who that self was once the friends were gone. The last time the West Side Gang and I got together, a few nights before my family left, we tried to say goodbye in our awkward way. Mike wanted me to stay there and live with him for my senior year, but I knew that wasn't possible. We all felt pretty gloomy.

"Hey, it's gonna be okay, Dave," Rick said. "You'll just finish your last year of school and then come back here. It'll still be the same, Dave—it'll always be the same." I wanted to believe him, but I simply couldn't.

I looked at him and said, "Rick, it's never gonna be the same." We sat there in silence as my eyes filled with tears. "Never the same."

Looking back, I see only one thing that opened the door to change in my life: moving. And I see only one person who could have orchestrated those circumstances at that precise time: God. Even before I cared one whit about him, he was taking care of me by removing me from the dead-end life I had been headed toward.

Of course, that was the last thing on my mind as our camper pulled away from our empty house in Missoula.

Shot put

PR: 50′1¾″

OK, I might as well just say it: I hate the shot put. It's boring. You're cramped. But you have to go through with it.

It's the first event that requires the use of an implement—the sixteen-pound shot. You have to heave or "put" it as far as you can from within a seven-foot circle. It requires a great deal of focused strength and explosiveness. When I step into the circle, I try to picture myself as a spring-loaded catapult, a weapon launcher. Every ounce of force must be concentrated in a straight line behind, and through, the shot in order to achieve maximum distance. A very strong athlete can have a poor throw if he fails to keep his energy in line.

In many ways it's an incredible event, but I still hate it. I don't like being confined to that circle. It's impossible to be graceful with a shot. It's ugly to look at and its flight is too short to appreciate. You start with a grunt, let out a scream as you release, and then listen for the thud. When you finish, the field is full of craters. In the discus or javelin you at least have the fun of watching the object fly through the air, and you're able to scream at it longer to make it go farther.

But the main reason I don't like the shot put is that it's one of my weakest events.

Isn't that true for all of us? We tend to dislike the things that are most difficult or uncomfortable or unglamorous. We don't like doing "grunt work." We don't like monotonous chores or duties that can only be done a certain way. And yet they are a necessary part of life, and they ask for our best effort. Not everything may come as easily to us as we like, but when we persevere and do it anyway, we build character in the process. We may even get better at it.

I try to remember that the shot put is only one out of ten events, but an essential one because the decathlon wouldn't exist without it. (I think they'd have to call it a "nonathlon.") In the same way, life wouldn't be normal without a few things we don't do well or don't like. Sometimes we simply need to get them out of the way—clear out the dead weight, if you will—and move on to the next task.

■ ■ ■

▪ chapter four ▪

GETTING ON TRACK

ENDINGS AND BEGINNINGS are often closely linked. Moving away from Missoula felt like a major ending for me. At one level I was trying to cope with the loss of my friends, but deeper down I struggled with the loss of what my friends meant to me: my sense of identity. They had always accepted me without question, so I never had to worry about saying or doing the wrong thing or being rejected. I never thought about my social skills or my appearance. Around them I could just be who I was and feel OK. When I left Missoula, the security I had felt in those friends came to an end.

But my arrival in Corvallis also signaled a new beginning. I'd have to find out who I was *apart* from the West Side Gang. I couldn't simply form a new group to hang out with, because I'd grown up with those guys; as I'd said to Rick, it just wouldn't be the same. Instead, for the first time, I'd have to rely on my own inner resources.

We lived in a relatively new neighborhood on the northeast side of town. Our house, originally a ranch style, had been converted into a two-story by adding two bedrooms and a bath above the attached garage. Lois had one room and I had the other—complete with blue shag carpet. We became quite close that summer and fall, and did a lot together because we didn't know many other people.

The city had two high schools—Corvallis High and Crescent Valley High. Corvallis High was a lot like Sentinel back in Missoula—sort of a working-class school. Kids wore flannel shirts, ignored fashion trends, and enjoyed a casual social life—the perfect place for me, in other words. Crescent Valley, on the other hand, was a modern, first-class facility where many of the more affluent kids went. Everybody wore preppy clothes, bought the "cool sneakers," and pursued a flashier social scene.

Guess where Lois and I went.

When I showed up for my first week at Crescent Valley, I quickly realized I was one of the messiest dressers on campus. In Missoula I'd never cared about what I wore to school, but here I discovered that the only guys who dressed like me were the cigarette smokers and the potheads. So I had to make awkward adjustments right away.

I had decided before the school year began that I'd go out for the football team in order to make some friends. That way I'd find the "right" crowd to hang out with, and have a better chance of meeting girls. I told the football coach that I was a wide receiver and that I'd played for several years in Montana—when, actually, I had never played organized football in my life. I also said I wanted to return punts and kickoffs. I think he believed me at first, but when he told me to run a few patterns or line up in certain formations, he soon figured out that I had no idea what to do. I usually bumbled my way through. He did see that I had natural athletic ability, however. I ran at least as fast as the other wide receivers, and I could catch the ball well. Because the other three guys had seniority, I had to settle for fourth-string receiver, but I did become the first-string kick returner.

Since I hadn't made any good friends yet, I poured my energy into working harder on the team, showing up for all the practices, persisting in the drills when others were goofing off, and taking extra time to work out in the weight room. I wasn't a loner or anything, at least on the outside; I made lots of casual friends and fit into the jock and party crowds. Many dating opportunities arose, probably because I was the new guy in town and a halfway-decent looking football player. And I have to admit that I more than took advantage of those opportunities. But inside, I was still afraid and insecure.

I got to know three guys during the football season. Terry, a running back, liked to smoke marijuana and go to parties, and he ushered me into the Crescent Valley social scene. Amit, the place-kicker, was a fun guy to hang around with, and occasionally I could talk to him. My third friend, Matt Hirte, was completely different. He, too, was a wide receiver, and since he was third string and I was fourth, we'd often stand on the sidelines together during games, as well as do the same routines in practice.

What made him different were the things we talked about. He didn't seem to care about the typical jock topics—women, drunken escapades, and pranks. Instead, he'd tell me about his spiritual life, something I'd never heard of, and about Christ, who I *had* heard of but rarely thought about. To Matt, Christ was not an abstract concept, but a living person you could talk to and learn from and draw strength from. Christ gave purpose and direction to his life, he said, and helped him to live in a positive way.

I thought he was pretty weird at first. People just don't talk about spirituality out of the blue—especially high school kids. But maybe that was the very reason I kept listening. Matt's faith obviously meant a lot to him, and it seemed to help him in his everyday life. The idea of having a *relationship* with God intrigued me. How could you have a relationship with someone you couldn't see—especially someone like God?

From time to time he'd ask me if I knew who Christ was, and whether I was happy with my life. Once he asked me if I thought I was going to heaven or hell. "Heaven, of course," I reacted. But in spite of these leading questions, he really didn't try to force religion on me. He truly wanted to be my friend, and he accepted me almost like the gang in Missoula had. Yet, he also felt free to talk about his beliefs. I was struck by the confidence his faith gave him.

Matt belonged to a Christian youth group in the area, and soon invited me to some of their functions, including church. I finally went to a youth group basketball night and had a good time. Before the game, the leader read something out of the Bible, talked about it briefly, and then said a prayer. The other kids seemed eager to learn about God and the Bible. Most of them acted like someone else was the center of the universe rather than themselves—a loving and powerful God who wanted to guide their lives. I began to be curious about who Jesus Christ was and whether he had anything to do with me.

Curiosity is one thing; change is quite another. At the same time I was exploring things of the spirit with Matt, I was also pursuing "spirits" with Terry—alcohol, that is. The parties we frequented always had plenty of beer, wine, and also marijuana, which I'd only tried once or twice in Missoula. So I began to smoke occasionally with Terry in addition to the drinking.

Rather than hide these habits from Matt, I'd ask him to join in.

"C'mon, Matt, we're gonna have a lot of fun tonight—we'll meet some girls."

The first time I asked him, his response caught me off guard.

"Thanks, Dave," he said, "but I don't need to do that. It's just not part of what I want to do with my life."

His honesty struck me, as did his clarity of purpose. He knew within himself that those activities would take his life in a direction he didn't want to go. And not only did he know it, but he was able to express it around his friends—something I'd never heard anybody do before. He didn't judge me or tell me I was going to hell because I wanted to party. He simply said *he* didn't want to. Of course, that didn't stop me from asking.

Eventually he did come a few times, but I noticed that he didn't drink or smoke pot; he'd just have a soda. He got along well with everyone and seemed to have a good time, yet he didn't need to get smashed. What a contrast to my own situation: I *couldn't* have fun unless I was getting wasted with the others. I was impressed by Matt's inner strength and poise, and actually began to look up to him as a person of integrity. I still invited him to parties, but never pressured him to drink or smoke.

Football season ended, and in early March track season would be starting. Matt and I kept up our friendship; I genuinely liked being around him. We continued to train together during the off-season, and I still went to youth group with him sometimes. As it turned out, Matt ran hurdles on the track team and encouraged me to join him. The football coach also happened to be the track coach, and he wanted me on the track team for my speed. I had only dabbled in track back in Missoula, but, largely because of Matt's influence, I decided to give it a shot.

Meanwhile, I was smoking marijuana with Terry and his friends more and more frequently—every weekend for sure, and often during the week, too. It got to the point where I was smoking pot more than I was drinking, and I began to feel some unnerving side effects.

On a typical weekend night I'd meet Terry and a couple of his friends, we'd smoke some pot, and head for a party. Once I got there, however, I felt increasingly unable to relate to anybody. If my first conversation with someone didn't go just right, I'd completely clam up for most of the night, afraid of saying something stupid and making a fool of myself. Or if I saw a group of people laughing across the room, I felt certain they were making fun of something I'd said. After this happened a few times, I developed major anxiety around other people.

Sometimes I'd go home after a party, still stoned, and sit in front of my bathroom mirror for maybe an hour, gazing at myself with glassy eyes. I'd feel weird about my body and my face and then I'd think, *What do people see when they look at my face?* At that time I had a little more acne than the average high school kid, which only fed my pot-induced paranoia, so I'd be even more convinced that people didn't like the way I looked—that is, they didn't like *me*. The next day of school those negative thoughts would stay with me, and if I saw a cluster of people I knew, I'd think, *I probably look as ugly to them now as I did to myself in the mirror the other night—I'd better not let them see me.* I worried that something was wrong with me, and became more withdrawn in groups.

I began to believe that all the marijuana was causing me to lose touch with reality. Most of my fears and worries arose from smoking pot, I realized, and I rarely had fun when I was high, so why did I keep doing it? Instead of helping me forget my problems and inadequacies, it caused me to focus on them all the more.

Before long, others noticed how gloomy I became when I smoked. A few times I skipped school in the morning and drove up into the mountains with Terry and his friends, where we sucked on a few joints, got philosophical, then went back to school for the rest of the day. One particular day one of Terry's friends decided he'd seen too many of my depressing episodes. He refused to let me come along because I'd spoil all the fun. Talk about adding insult to injury. I understood his reasons, but I felt so rejected. I was becoming afraid of what this weed was doing to me.

I also began to fear for my life. One Saturday night, after heavy smoking and drinking at a party until three in the morning, Terry and I climbed into the cab of a big four-wheel-drive pickup for the ride home. Two other guys jumped in the back, and Barry, the driver, walked up with the keys. As he opened the door to get in, I had an idea—a safety idea.

"Dude," I said, "We've been drinking and smoking a lot, and you're gonna drive pretty fast because this is your truck and you're used to how it feels. Why don't you let me drive? I'll be more careful because it's not my car and then maybe we'll make it home."

"Oh Dave, don't worry, I'll be OK," Barry said, overconfidently. He revved the truck's V–8 engine and squealed the tires as we took off. I didn't have a good feeling about this ride home. Moments later we were doing 60 on a winding 40-mph road that skirted the side of a hill. Barry foolishly decided he wanted to take out mailboxes, so he'd swerve off the road, bowl over a few with the truck's huge grille, and swing back onto the pavement again. But after doing this once or twice, we hit some gravel and skidded sideways. Barry struggled to regain control as the truck lurched back and forth, but to no avail.

When I felt the back end slip over the edge of the road and pull us downward, I knew this was serious. Below was a steep slope that leveled off into a field. For some reason I knew that as soon as we hit bottom, the truck would roll. Instinctively, I grabbed underneath the dashboard and held on to keep from hitting the roof.

As the truck rolled—six or seven times in all—I could hear the shattering of glass and the crashing of metal. The bouncing headlight beams made circles in the night like searchlights.

"Oh my God," I said on the way down. I almost never used that phrase or meant it, but this time I was actually thinking about God, as if I were going to be facing him at any moment.

The next thing I knew I was flying through the air. Somehow I had been ejected from the truck, and it seemed like I was floating. But I had a sense of where the ground was, so I simply tucked my head in, landed on my shoulder, took one somersault, and came up on my feet—just like the times I'd tumbled down the stairs as a kid. I had a little scrape on my arm from sliding in the dirt, but nothing else.

I looked over at the truck, which had finally come to rest on its side. The cab where I'd been sitting was crushed completely flat, level with the hood. All was silent.

Suddenly feeling sober and alert, I called out, "You guys all right?"

One by one we found each other. One of the two guys in back had been thrown clear and suffered only a sore back. The other had torn up his hands badly from gripping the edge of the truck. Terry cracked a vertebra in his neck and had a concussion, but I was able to help him up to the road. That left Barry, the driver. After looking around in the darkness, we found him lying in the bushes forty or fifty feet away from the truck, unconscious. He'd taken a major blow to the head. When the ambulance arrived—a man from a nearby mobile home had called—we were all taken to the hospital.

Exactly how I got out of that truck, especially with no cuts or bruises, I'll never know. I honestly think that God yanked me from that cab and tossed me out of the way. He was protecting me for some reason. And in spite of the others' injuries, it was miraculous that we weren't all killed. My parents must have realized this, because they were extremely glad to see me when they arrived at the hospital to pick me up.

I eventually stopped hanging around with Terry and his buddies. And because of the physical danger as well as the emotional torment pot smoking was causing me, I cut way back on the stuff.

My last significant pot experience occurred on the way to a concert in Portland. I didn't care about the music; I went because a girl I'd been dating was going. A bunch of us had piled into a van for the two-hour drive, and we smoked the whole way. It was a "bad trip" in more ways than one: The same fear and mental turmoil returned, and I could tell my girlfriend noticed I was getting weird. I was so scared to talk I just sat there in silent anguish. I remember wishing that my old buddies from the West Side Gang were around, so I could know who I was and feel good about that person. By the time I got home, I was utterly miserable. I even quit dating the girl afterwards; one of the other guys on the trip started going out with her.

I only smoked a couple of times after that, and only with one or two people. Then one day I simply decided, *This is it.* From that point on, when someone asked me to smoke with them, I'd say, "No thanks, I'm not gonna do that anymore." People found it a little strange to see me taking a stand, but I didn't care. It actually felt good to say no to something that had been messing me up so much. That three-month period had nearly ruined my life—nearly *ended* my life—and I was glad to be out from under it. The effects on my confidence and self-esteem, however, would last for years.

■ ■ ■

By now track season had begun. I hung out mostly with Matt, Amit, and Jim, another guy on the track team. I liked being around them because they didn't seem to care about my lack of social skills. Though I'd put down the pot, I still kept up the drinking, and Jim and I became great drinking buddies. I even talked Matt into having a beer with us once in a while. If we went to a party afterwards, I'd keep on drinking, however, while Matt simply stopped. My fear and insecurity around other people relaxed somewhat.

In the meantime, we were trying to get in shape for track and practice our events. Matt and I worked on the intermediate and high hurdles, and I couldn't believe how naturally they came to me. In about two weeks I was "three-stepping" between the hurdles (most beginners take five), and shortly after that I was beating Matt. I also tried the high jump and joined Jim on the mile relay, picking them up so quickly that I beat most of my teammates.

The season went extremely well, and I had a great time. Our mile relay team placed second in the district and fourth in the state. And I was the top hurdler and the top high jumper on the team.

Shortly after the big district meet, I got a phone call from the track coach at Linn-Benton Community College in Albany, about ten miles from Corvallis. His name was David Bakley, and he said he'd seen me at the meet. He was a friendly guy, and thought I had a lot of potential to excel in track and field. He wondered if I'd made my college plans yet, and said he'd love to work with me if I'd consider coming to Linn-Benton in the fall.

Then he asked me if I'd ever considered trying the decathlon.

"Oh, you mean marathon?" I said. I'd never heard the word *decathlon* before, so I figured he had mispronounced "marathon." I wasn't a distance runner, so I couldn't imagine why he'd be asking me about the marathon.

"No, I mean *decathlon*," he reiterated. "You know, with the ten events—what Bruce Jenner did at the Olympics."

Bruce Jenner. That name rang a bell.

"Oh, yeah—he's the guy on 'CHiPS,' right?" I had seen him on the show a few times, and vaguely remembered that he had done sports before getting into acting.

"Well, yes," Dave said, "but before that he won the gold medal in the decathlon at the Olympics in '76. Remember the victory lap he ran while carrying the American flag? And his face on the Wheaties boxes?"

Yeah, sort of.

He went on to describe each of the ten events in a decathlon. I already did the hurdles, the high jump, and the 400 meters (one leg of the mile relay), but I'd never tried most of the others. It sounded difficult, but also challenging. He told me I had the right kind of body for a decathlete. At the time I was 6'2" and around 170 lbs.—a little on the skinny side. If I lifted weights and built up my muscles, he said, I could do very well in the decathlon.

I can't say I had this immediate desire to do the decathlon. But during that short conversation, something about Dave Bakley made a significant impression on me. He wasn't merely trying to be a salesman for his college. He saw something in me, a raw talent that could be nurtured and developed under the right circumstances. I thanked him for calling me, and said I'd think about what he said.

My track accomplishments gave a strong boost to my flagging self-esteem. I'd been feeling so inept socially that I wondered whether I could do anything right. To discover—or maybe *re*discover—that I was good at something made such a difference. I'd already competed well in football, but since I'd never really done track before, my high scores seemed much more significant. Suddenly, here I was, the best hurdler and high jumper in my school for that year. The achievement caught me completely by surprise; it was too good to be merely coincidental. It felt less like something I'd earned and more like something that had been provided for me. I'd worked hard for it, certainly, but I also sensed a larger Presence at work—something or someone who wanted to be involved in my life. I wondered if this Presence had anything to do with the God I'd been hearing about from Matt and from the youth group basketball nights I'd been attending.

As the school year wound down, I realized I'd made no plans for my life after graduation. I really hadn't thought much about my future, although I'd half-heartedly sent out a few applications back in the fall. Matt and I had talked about going to Willamette University in Salem, but it didn't work out. For some reason I now felt a new motivation to go to college. I started checking on schools in the area, including Oregon State and Linn-Benton, which were less than fifteen minutes from my house. Even though I'd appreciated the phone call from Coach Bakley at Linn-Benton, the school had no football team, which to me was a strike against it. I resolved to keep looking.

I also kept wondering about the place of God in my life. I'd heard Matt talk about Jesus Christ many times, but I'd never taken the time to find out for myself what it all meant. And the positive experience I was having in track only increased my curiosity. The more youth group events I frequented with Matt, the more I saw that it was Christ who made it possible for the people there to have a good time and feel a stronger sense of their identity as Christians. At least that's what they were saying, and something about it rang true for me. I found myself being drawn closer to making a connection with Christ.

I hadn't yet grasped some of the fuller implications of turning my life over to God, however. Outside of the youth group, I continued my drinking and partying, and I still fooled around with girls. Late in the spring, the youth group sponsored its own Beach Olympics on the ocean, and Matt invited me to go. In great shape from track, I won the whole contest. But I couldn't resist trying to pick up some of the girls there— as I'd already done on several occasions at the youth center. I'm sure I corrupted more than a few of them.

Nevertheless, I talked to more people and asked more questions about Christianity. Rather than listen and reflect, as I'd done with Matt, I now took the initiative. One guy I approached was Kurt Spence, who attended youth group and also went to Crescent Valley. I had pegged him as kind of a nerd since he didn't do any sports, but he knew all about Christ and the Bible, so I began talking to him often about what it meant to be a Christian.

Matt had done an incredible job of arousing my interest in Christ, and simply caring about me as a friend. Kurt, on the other hand, was a man on a mission to get me "saved." Actually his style, which was sometimes harsh and abrupt, bugged me at first. He kept telling me to quit drinking, and that I'd go to hell if I didn't accept Christ. By now I knew the "external" steps a person needed to take if he wanted to invite Christ into his life, but I still didn't feel ready on the inside to take those steps.

Kurt introduced me to Ron, one of the leaders of the youth group. He was probably ten years older, and he invited me to dinner at his home with a bunch of his older Christian friends. Based on the lingo they used and the way they prayed around me, I got the feeling that they were trying to reel me into the fold. Their approach turned me off, but I didn't give up on my spiritual search. The Lord was working on me in his own way.

Sometime in July, Ron took me for a ride along the Willamette River outside of Corvallis. He had simply told me we were going to go floating on the river. After parking the car, we walked upstream on a bicycle path for two or three miles. Then we waded into the cool water and started floating back— just the two of us, no inner tubes or vests or anything. He'd done it many times, and told me not to worry. Though the river was relatively calm and free of rapids, the current ran fairly strong. Where we started, I could simply lift my feet and take off. When I got a little tired, I'd touch bottom again, then lift my feet and go, then touch, then go, and so on. I enjoyed it at first—a real live experience of "going with the flow."

Eventually we drifted out toward the middle, where the river deepened and I could no longer touch bottom. Suddenly things weren't quite as enjoyable. For a stretch of at least a mile, I had to work much harder to tread water and stay afloat—so hard, in fact, that I struggled to keep my head above water. A few times I nearly panicked, but I managed to maintain my composure.

Meanwhile, Ron remained nearby, floating almost effortlessly in the current. I guess he *had* done this before; he appeared to be an excellent swimmer. I was tired and desperately wanted to move over to the shallower water, but I didn't want him to know it. I wouldn't move unless he did. I sensed that he was testing me, perhaps to see how much nerve I had, or how much athletic ability, or how much willingness to entrust my life to another person. But if he intended to scare me, he did. When we finally reached the end and climbed onto the riverbank, I collapsed on the ground, exhausted. Ron looked genuinely surprised that I'd made it the whole way without his help.

I realized he had indeed tried to scare me. His plan? If I'd nearly drowned and then allowed him to save me, maybe it would have broken down my self-sufficiency and helped me see more vividly my need for Christ. He didn't say as much, but I'm pretty sure that's what was going on inside his head.

There on the bank, we sat down and he started to pray aloud.

"Thank you, Lord, for this beautiful day, for this river and its refreshing water . . . Thank you for this time with Dave, and for all that you're doing in his life. . . ."

I didn't pay close attention to his words, because I was still recovering from the tortuous trip. My heart was still pounding and I felt very weak.

Then he closed his prayer by saying, "Lord, I'd like to open up this prayer now for anything Dave might want to say to you."

We sat there in silence, our heads bowed. Two, three, four, five minutes passed and I said nothing. I didn't like being pressured to pray or to "accept Christ," and I felt self-conscious about the whole day's experience. He wanted me to make a commitment right then, and I still didn't feel ready. I needed to know that my motivation was coming from within me rather than from others.

But I also knew it wasn't simply a matter of feeling ready. Some part of me was resisting the urge to say yes to God. Maybe I didn't fully understand what it would mean for my life. The other kids in the youth group seemed different because they had turned their lives over to Christ, but I wasn't sure *why* they were different, or what it was that Christ did for them.

Finally Ron gave up and closed the prayer. "Thanks again, Lord, for this day. Amen." He started to get up.

"Wait a minute," I blurted out. "I need to say a little prayer."

He sat back down.

In a shaky voice, I said only one short sentence: "Dear Lord, please don't ever give up on me."

That was it. The first time I'd ever prayed out loud—not counting the moments I'd gasped for God's help when I was about to get caught for something I'd done. I simply wanted to tell God—or maybe myself—that I was *trying* to learn what faith was all about, and *trying* to accept Christ and his truth into my life. In spite of the awkward circumstances, it represented a major step for me. I felt like my meager prayer bounced off Ron, shot up to the Lord, and came back down to me as a solid confirmation that I was moving closer to Jesus Christ.

Over the next few weeks I hung around the youth center a lot and paid much closer attention during the Bible studies. I also read from my mom's old Catholic Bible at home. I was learning all kinds of things from Scripture, from the group leaders, and from the other kids who seemed to feel so good about who they were and where they were going because Christ was in their lives.

They seemed so much freer than I did. The more time I spent with them, the more I sensed a heaviness in myself that they didn't seem to have. I felt the weight of my past, as well as guilt for all the trouble I'd caused my parents, other people, and myself. Guilt for thrashing all those houses and gardens. Guilt for defying and lying to my parents and the police. Guilt for all the alcohol and other things I'd stolen. Guilt for terrorizing that little boy and others over the years. I didn't want to carry that weight around with me any more; I wanted to leave it behind and give my life a fresh start, to go forward with my life in a positive direction, to feel confident in who I was and in the person I was becoming.

I knew these other kids weren't perfect or blissfully happy or free from all problems. To the contrary, they often talked about their problems and their wrongdoings; but they saw God as someone who gave them help and forgiveness for those problems. Overall they sure seemed a lot freer and "lighter" and more inner-directed than I was. And it was through Christ that they had found that freedom and purpose. So, finally, one day I went up to Kurt Spence at the youth center.

"Kurt, I think I'm ready to bring Christ into my life."

He smiled. I knew he'd been hoping and praying for this moment, and it seemed right to go to him.

"Let's take a walk and get away from all these people," he said.

We went over to a nearby park and sat down on one of the benches. Again he explained to me what it meant to trust my life to Christ, and then we prayed. Following his lead, I thanked God for loving me, and for sending Jesus Christ to die on the cross. I asked Jesus to take away my sins and forgive me for hurting others. Finally I asked him to take charge of my life and make me into the person he wanted me to be.

It's amazing how powerful a decision can be when you make it on your own and for your own reasons—not because someone's pressured you or made you feel obligated. I said yes to Christ not because I wanted to impress people or fit into a certain group, but because *I* realized *my* need for him. If I had given in earlier to the "Christian peer pressure" I was feeling from some people at the youth center, my choice may not have meant nearly as much. Fortunately, I was able to accept Christ in a way that would be meaningful to me.

Now that I'd made the choice, I felt the heaviness being lifted. In its place came a freshness, as if a huge wave had swept through my body and washed everything clean. Now I could start over again and rebuild my life on a solid foundation. I felt inspired to make the most of the mind and body God had given me. I wanted to set goals for my life.

I shook Kurt's hand and we walked back to the youth center. He was happy for me and started telling Ron and the other directors and a few kids. As they warmly congratulated me, I felt a little embarrassed because I didn't like being the center of attention. But mostly I felt thankful to God and confident that he was going to do great things in my life.

From that point forward I wanted to conquer the world, and my first move in that direction was college. I arranged to attend Western Oregon State in Monmouth, where I'd be able to play football. I was all fired up to make a difference in college; I wanted to lead Bible studies and tell others about my faith. So I asked Kurt to work with me and help me get ready to be a strong Christian at WOSC.

I'd invite him over to my house, where we'd talk about the Lord and study the Bible up in my room. My parents, especially Mom, wondered why Kurt was hanging around so much because he was so different than any of the other friends I'd brought home. When they saw us reading the Bible, they grew suspicious at first, almost as if I'd joined a cult. I hadn't really explained to them what had happened to me. I felt awkward about it because we had never talked about spiritual issues or read the Bible together. They never criticized me for it, but they did seemed concerned.

"What are you guys doing?" Mom finally asked one day.

"Well, we're having a Bible study," I said. "I've become a Christian. I've accepted Christ into my life."

She looked perplexed. "What are you talking about?" she said. "You already know him." In her mind I was already a Christian since I'd been baptized in the Catholic church. If that was true, I wondered, why had I never known I was a Christian before? I didn't know how to explain to her that I wasn't turning my back on Catholicism or minimizing its value; I had simply discovered anew that Jesus was a real person who I could have a relationship with, someone who could change my life.

Before long she and Dad began to feel happy for me. They both saw that I was changing. I was treating them with more love and respect, and instead of ignoring them or refusing to tell them anything, I tried to share more freely with them what was going on in my life. They also noticed I was beginning to hang out with a different, more positive group of people who didn't get into trouble, which sure made Dad breathe easier.

I never really told Matt about my becoming a Christian either, though he had heard it from others. Something had happened that summer—I'm not sure what—between him and me: We drifted apart. I don't remember either of us hurting or offending the other. I think that at the same time I was zeroing in on Christ, Matt was entering a period of questioning his faith. By the end of the summer, we had pretty much gone our separate ways.

We have run into each other a few times over the years, but never long enough to catch up on everything. I hope to have that opportunity soon. In high school we had joked with each other on occasion that one day he'd be a rock singer/songwriter, and I'd be a track star. A few years later he said one day he'd give me backstage passes to his concerts and that I could give him tickets to the Olympic Games. Maybe in 1996 I'll be able to do that.

In any case, I will always be grateful to Matt for befriending me and for expressing to me in a natural way who God was to him. I marvel sometimes at the kinds of people God frequently chooses to work through. Rarely are they the perfect, totally together types. More often they're just ordinary people who may be struggling with doubts, like Matt. Or out-of-control kids with rough edges, like me.

Senior year of high school: a very up-and-down year in which I felt some of my lowest lows and my highest highs—in more ways than one. But during that year three significant things occurred that set the stage for my future as a decathlete: I began to clean up my life (emphasis on *began*); I excelled in track for the first time; and with the help of two special friends, I found God. Even though I'd still have lots of areas to work on, I had crossed an important line—between darkness and light—and there was no turning back. The concurrent timing of all these events had such a profound effect on me that even today I am constantly struck by the parallels between my life as a Christian and my life as an athlete.

High Jump
PR: 6'10¾"

For the first time I must overcome a visible obstacle—a bar. It is my adversary: it gives me no encouragement, has no sense of humor, and never forgives. It simply glares at me from its perch at least six feet skyward, daring me to get in its way.

I am given no implements to help me get over this bar—no pole, no springboard. All I have is my own body, my own self. Every resource for defeating this enemy must come from within.

The bar events are amazing to me. The high jump is the most incredible of all, and the pole vault isn't far behind. To gain both the elevation and the coordination needed to clear a bar is an incredible athletic achievement.

In making the actual jump, I approach somewhat slowly from the right side, carefully noting my steps. Then I suddenly push off from my left leg as hard as I can, turn away from the bar, and arch my back. After gaining enough height, at just the right moment I clear my legs and feet and flop into the pit on the back of my neck. Sounds simple, right?

But when you stand before that bar, your first impulse is to say, "No way. I can't do this." In the other events, you still get points for a slow race or a weak throw. But you can't have a weak jump. You either make it or you don't. And if you don't, you can kiss goodbye any chances of winning a major competition. Once you clear that opening height, however, you've earned some points and you can relax—but only a little. The bar moves in only one direction: up.

Unlike the other eight events, in which you don't know the outcome until afterwards, the bar events give you all the facts up front. You see the goal you have to reach. You know what your score will be if you make it—or if you don't. These facts pose a different kind of mental challenge than the non-bar events.

In addition to the imposing bar and the extreme concentration required to clear it, another mental and physical challenge is the long waiting between jumps. The whole event can easily last four hours, sometimes five. You have two minutes to take each jump, and three attempts at each height. You jump and then wait for all the others to take their turn. Hopefully, you'll be able to conserve energy by taking the fewest jumps possible. But if you miss your first two jumps, then make the third, then do the same thing for the next couple of heights, you'll be pretty exhausted by the time it's all over. Including warmups, you could take as many as fifteen jumps.

A positive way to look at the high jumping—and life—is to realize the need to set specific, concrete goals, but also realizable ones. We all have times when we must face a seemingly impossible task. We take one look and tell ourselves, "I'll never be able to do this." But remember, you don't start with the bar at seven feet. You begin much lower and work your way up. Then, as you accomplish your intermediate goals, your confidence builds until one day you discover you have the inner resources needed to succeed. Some of the most satisfying moments you will ever experience occur when you finally take that last leap and realize you've reached a height you never thought would be attainable.

■ ■ ■

∎ chapter five ∎

RAW POTENTIAL

ONCE I MADE a commitment to God, everything in my life came together. In the fall of 1981 at Western Oregon State, I grew spiritually in leaps and bounds, led dormitory Bible studies, lived an exemplary Christian lifestyle, and became a star on the football team.

Not.

Actually, I floundered. I hardly saw Kurt after the school year began. I didn't lead any Bible studies; I didn't even read the Bible. And I didn't look for a church or a Christian group on campus to get involved in. I knew that my faith was real and alive somewhere inside of me, but I hadn't yet learned how to develop a day-by-day relationship with Christ.

The only concrete way I knew to express my faith was through sports. Because I was a Christian, I told myself, I was going to give one hundred percent for the Lord. I was going to work my butt off for the football team. And believe me, I did. I pushed myself harder than all the other freshmen and most of the upperclassmen. When we did wind sprints, for instance—running a full hundred yards and back five times in a row—I'd go full speed, while the other guys would slow down and pace themselves. I'd run myself into the dirt, nearly puking in pain, but I'd always be the first one to finish. Each week I got faster and finished farther ahead of everyone. "Good job, Dave," the coaches would say when they noticed my effort.

The season went well. As a freshman, I was consigned to the JV team, but I started every game and had lots of playing time. I wasn't afraid to make the catch and take the hit. I could outrun many of the defensive backs from other teams, and several times I was able to haul in a long bomb. I was thrilled to catch my first touchdown pass—I squeezed the ball so hard I thought I would pop it.

There was one thing that put a damper on the whole season, however: I never played in a varsity game. Not one. Not even one play.

It was mostly an issue of seniority. The varsity receivers were upperclassmen and had more experience, so they deserved to play ahead of me, even though I was probably as good as they were. But I had trained so hard in practice, and performed so well on the field, that I felt sure the coaches would at least ask me to join the varsity travel team at some point and perhaps go in for a few plays.

They didn't.

By the end of the season, I was pretty angry at the coaches and at the whole seniority system. So angry, in fact, that I decided not to return to Western Oregon State. I'd finish out the year and then go somewhere else. I'm not sure why it was so important to me to play in a varsity game. I think that even though I was confident in my athletic ability, I needed some kind of adult recognition at that particular time. I needed someone to say, "I believe in you." I honestly think that if I'd been able to play in just one varsity game, I would have stayed at WOSC, played football four years, and probably pursued a football career.

But it was not meant to be.

Even after football season was over, I continued to hang around mostly with guys from the team. I felt comfortable around them because they respected me for my athletic ability. At that point sports was still the only area of my life in which I felt confident; outside that arena the same old insecurity would return. I hadn't yet become grounded enough in my faith that I could draw upon God for my sense of worth.

Though I never fooled around with marijuana or drugs again, I continued my old habit of drinking and partying regularly. My roommate, Joe Harmon, had graduated with me from Crescent Valley, and we became good buddies. He and I and a couple of other guys started our own group—not really a troublemaking group, outside of a few pranks, but more of a drinking group. The idea came about in a pretty sick way. One night we had been drinking and were sitting outside our dorm near a small pond when we decided that the croaking of the frogs was bugging us. We set out to catch some of them.

As we hunted around the edge of the pond, someone said, "Hey, let's start a group and call ourselves the Frog Catchers— no one can be a member unless he catches a frog."

Good idea, we decided, but catching a frog was too easy. What about *killing* a frog? Better, but the deed needed to pose a special challenge. Another minute of brainstorming and we had it: Anyone who wanted to join the group would have to kill a frog by biting its head off. Yes, that would do it. (Talk about a nasty taste. I can see it on the appetizer menu now: "Crown of Amphibian, *au jus*.") We came up with the perfect name for ourselves, too: The Riptiles.

To announce our group to the whole school, one of the guys painted a flag on a pillow case with a bloody frog's head and "The Riptiles" underneath. Then we climbed to the top of a tall evergreen tree on campus and attached it to the top, where it hung for several weeks until someone from the school could get it down.

I also got in trouble again over Christmas break. In late fall I had begun to get ready for the winter track season. (Meets are held indoors during the winter, and outdoors in the spring.) During my workouts I had made a new friend, a long jumper from Nigeria who would become one of my very best friends in college. His African name was Babajide, but everyone called him Jide. School was closed for the holidays, and Jide was visiting me at my home in Corvallis. While we were together, I decided that I needed something from my dorm room back at WOSC. We made the thirty-minute drive only to find all the campus buildings completely locked. With my past experience breaking into houses, however, I figured I could slip into my room through a window. We didn't even have to break it; we were able to push on the seal, pop the window off, climb in, and get what I needed. That was it. No stealing. No thrashing. Unfortunately, however, the police were waiting for us outside the building, and we were hauled in for breaking and entering into my own room. In order to keep the "crime" off our record, we had to sign a diversion agreement and promise not to break the law for a year.

■   ■   ■

Slowly, I began to redirect some of my negative energy into more positive activities. I continued working on my track skills. I told the track coach that Coach Bakley at Linn-Benton had suggested I try the decathlon, so he got me started on learning the events. Many of them were completely new: I'd never pole vaulted or thrown a discus or a shot. They seemed awfully hard at first. But I thrived on the challenge of learning something new, and spent many January and February days practicing in the indoor workout area beneath the stadium.

Even more than learning the events, I loved the rush of *improving*. As the season got underway, it seemed that each week I did better than the last, and the higher numbers drove me to work even harder. In the pole vault, for instance, I started off at nine feet, then a week later cleared ten feet, then eleven feet the next. From that point, it seemed like I improved a foot a month for the next four or five months. When I first tried the discus, several other guys could throw it farther, but after four or five months I was bettering their distances by ten to fifteen feet. Then there was the javelin: I ended up throwing it more than 200 feet, a freshman school record.

It amazed me that I was excelling so quickly and so natu- rally—even more so than in high school track. It got to the point that every time I tried a new event, I soon became one of the best on the team and would have to compete in it at dual meets. In fact, I was afraid to do well in the 1500 meters, because then I'd have to run it every week.

My very first decathlon took place in March, 1982, at Willamette University in Salem. I scored 6297, not bad for my debut. I don't remember much about the meet except that my parents were there and they couldn't figure out why I wanted to compete in the decathlon. I also remember standing in awe of the winner, Greg Hanson of Willamette, who scored in the 6800s. Little did I know that he would later offer me a piece of advice that would change the direction of my life.

Throughout the season I felt even more strongly what I'd experienced the year before on the Crescent Valley track team: a feeling of gratitude to God for watching over me and giving me this special ability in track. I knew he had allowed it to happen for a reason. When I had moved to Oregon, I had lost my sense of identity, and now God was providing a way to get it back—most importantly, through Jesus, and now through the sport of track and field.

Off the track, I continued to struggle with insecurity around other people. For one thing, I felt very self-conscious about my acne. When I looked in the mirror and saw a blemish, I wanted to get rid of it so bad that I scratched and picked and made it worse. I will always have scars on my face from that period of my life. I already worried too much about what others thought of me, and in my mind a face full of zits would only make matters worse.

Combine that with my lack of confidence in my communication skills, and I was one paranoid guy. Sometimes while I talked with people I'd say something and then get so wrapped up in what they thought of me that I'd lose track of the conversation. Then one of them would turn to me and say, "So what do you think, Dave?" and I'd be caught in a worse dilemma: If I said "What were you talking about?" then they'd know I wasn't listening and I'd look like a geek. But if I faked it and offered an answer, I'd risk looking even more stupid. Situations like these caused me to withdraw from everyone just like I had when I smoked marijuana. And people noticed.

The process of my becoming a solid Christian was slow, awkward, and full of contradictions. I felt God's presence, and my own sense of worth, but only in relation to sports. I wanted to get to know Christ better; I wanted him to affect my whole life. But I didn't yet have Christians around me who could help me grow spiritually, and I simply wasn't strong enough to seek them out or to survive on my own. To most my friends that year it probably didn't look like my lifestyle had changed at all. In many ways it hadn't. But even as I drank and partied, I always felt that Christ was still within me, waiting patiently for me to give all of my life to him. I knew he had heard my prayer by the river the previous summer: He wouldn't give up on me.

■   ■   ■

Somehow I managed to make it through the school year. After doing so well in track, part of me wanted to stay at Western Oregon State. I'd made some good friends, and I wanted to room with Joe Harmon again. He was a psychology major, and as he'd told me about his classes during the year I'd become fascinated with the field and decided to study it myself. It would have been fun to be roommates and psych majors together. But something inside was telling me to leave. I still hadn't gotten football out of my system, and I was too ticked off at the WOSC coaches to play for them. I felt unsettled, restless, unsure of my next step. I needed to get away for a while.

That summer I rode with my parents to North Dakota. My grandpa had recently died, and Grandma needed some help with the farm, so I decided to stay on with her while I figured out what to do in the fall. On the way out there, we stopped in Missoula, and I got together with Mike and some of my old friends. It was great to see them, but I had been right—it wasn't the same. When I told them about the decathlon and showed them pictures of me hurdling and pole vaulting, they thought I was a little strange. Why in the world would I want to be like that guy on "CHiPS"?

While in North Dakota, I built a fence for my grandma, fixed up some furniture, and did other repair and maintenence work around the farm. I also helped her get her driver's license. She'd been driving around the farm for years, but she'd never taken the test to drive on the roads. So I sat down with her and the motor vehicle book and helped her memorize everything she needed for the test. At the age of seventy-five, she passed it the very first time.

To keep in shape, I ran several miles nearly every day. Much of the credit for my conditioning that summer went to the millions of mosquitoes that constantly swarmed about; they would only light and bite when I slowed down, so I ran fast in order to stay ahead of them. I was hoping I might be able to land a scholarship somewhere. My sister Barb and her husband, Roger Smith, had recently moved to Bozeman, Montana, and I wondered about going to Montana State University there. I contacted the coach about playing football, but he made no offers other than to say I was welcome to try out for the team. When I mentioned some of my track scores and asked about a track scholarship, he didn't seem particularly impressed. He'd have to get back to me, he said.

Not very promising, but it was worth a try. Catching a ride to Bozeman (I had no car), I arranged to stay with Barb and Roger for a few months to earn some college money. Then, if the scholarship worked out, I'd be able to jump right into the spring semester, which began in January.

I enjoyed being with Barb and Roger. They'd always been accepting of me, even when I was regularly getting myself into trouble. I'd gone to Roger several times in high school after I'd drunk too much and gotten myself into a jam. Once I had stupidly driven Dad's pickup into an open field, only to get hopelessly stuck in the mud. When I called Roger, he didn't judge me, but came right over and helped me pull it out. I'm sure he must have thought I was a spoiled snot at times, but he and Barb never stopped caring about me. They also were Christians, and even though we didn't talk a lot about our faith, I felt comfortable around them.

As it turned out, steady work was scarce in the area, and all three of us had to grab any job we could find. Barb worked part-time in a shoe store, and Roger was helping a local contractor build a church. He talked the foreman into hiring me, so we could drive to work together. In addition, Roger and I spent several evenings a week assembling wood stoves and pre-fab greenhouses for a metal shop. We worked hard and put in long hours, often not getting home until midnight. After the church construction wound down, I pestered the manager of a truck stop restaurant for several weeks until he gave me a job as a waiter. I was the first male waiter there, and many of the truckers didn't quite know what to think of me. I took it all in good humor, though the tips could have been better.

It occurred to me that these were the first "real" jobs I'd ever had—not counting my brief high school stints in Missoula. Now I was actually trying to earn and save money for college. The work was tedious, but I liked taking responsibility for myself and being independent for the first time. Even though the three of us often ate egg-salad-and-tuna sandwiches for lunch and macaroni and cheese for dinner, we survived.

Amid the busy work schedule Roger and I also found time to run four or five times a week. I had plotted a course that snaked around town for about five miles before we'd arrive back home again. For the last 400 yards or so, I'd always say, "OK, let's race!" and I'd take off at full tilt, leaving Roger in the dust.

Several times he gave me a ride over to Montana State so I could check in with the coach. For some unknown reason, the coach didn't seem very interested in me. We walked out to the track one day and stood talking under the scoreboard, where all the school athletic records were inscribed. The track records weren't all that impressive.

Reading a few numbers off the board, I said, "Coach, I can beat those records."

"That's nice," he answered flatly.

I should have known right then that this guy wouldn't be any help to me, but I still held on to the irrational hope that he'd come through.

He didn't.

After going home with Barb and Roger to Oregon for Christmas, I returned with them to Montana, thinking I'd be going to school there. Not only were there no messages from the coach, all the scholarship application dates had passed as well. I hadn't even been given the courtesy of a return phone call.

That was it. Now I had to make some fast decisions. Taking the money I'd earned, I bought myself a car—a brown 1971 Pontiac Grand Ville with a big engine. It cost me exactly one thousand dollars. After Roger and I had installed a nice sound system, I said good-bye to him and Barb and headed back to Corvallis. If I hustled, I could still enroll at Linn-Benton Community College for the spring semester. At least their track coach, Dave Bakley, had seemed interested in me. As soon as I got home, I picked up the phone.

"Coach Bakley? This is Dave Johnson. Remember me?"

"Of course I do, Dave," he responded immediately. "How've you been?"

We didn't talk long, but he indicated that he knew all about how well I'd done at Western Oregon State, and that he'd be excited for me to come to Linn-Benton. I went over to see him a day or two later.

Like many community colleges, the Linn-Benton campus had a modern, sterile feel. Fortunately, Coach Bakley did not. He greeted me warmly and invited me to sit down in the soft armchair in his office. On the wall was a poster with the words "Be Alive." I filled him in on my successes and frustrations during the year and a half since we'd first talked. He listened closely and looked me right in the eyes. He clearly seemed to care about me—not merely as an athlete, but as a person. Almost immediately, he picked up on my confusion and vulnerability, and made it clear that he wanted to help me find the sense of direction I was looking for.

Right away we got to work on the decathlon. Coach Bakley was an excellent technician; he could pinpoint the precise adjustments needed for me to improve in each event, especially the pole vault. He was also tough on us: he pushed us to give everything we had and more—to go *beyond* what we thought we could do. It was a positive, motivating kind of toughness that arose not from a power trip, but from his special ability to see our potential and help us believe we could reach it. At the same time, he didn't take it all too seriously; he told us we shouldn't be doing track at all unless we could have fun, too.

I practiced hard. Again I felt that same addiction to improving as I'd felt at Western Oregon State, and the more I pushed myself, the better I got. When practices wound down for the day, I'd keep right on working until I was the last guy on the field. Coach Bakley didn't want to dampen my enthusiasm, I'm sure, but he also wanted to teach me not to obsess about sports. Every time he'd tell me to knock off, I'd say, "OK, Coach—just one more throw." Or jump. Or sprint. On many occasions he finally had to issue a direct order: "Look, Dave— I'm leaving. I'm out of here, and you need to be out of here too. We're *done.*"

Coach seemed to be as concerned about the rest of our lives as he did about our athletic lives. He was very "whole person centered" in his approach, and he reminded us to keep sports in perspective. When it comes to the grand scheme of things, he would say, athletics aren't all that important. What's most important, he'd emphasize, is who you are as a human being. He always encouraged us to stick with our classes, keep our grades up (which I actually did!), and stay emotionally healthy. I liked his way of coaching. Not only did it help me tremendously, but it also fit with my fledgling faith.

I first learned from him how much one's emotional state can affect athletic performance. He had the uncanny ability to discern very quickly how we were feeling about ourselves on a given day simply by reading our posture, our body language, our facial expressions. In the decathlon, he taught me how to deal with failure and success in each event. If I did poorly in one event, he'd tell me to let myself feel bad about it—for two minutes. Then he had me ask myself, "OK, what can I learn from this and how can I improve next time?" Finally, I needed to let it go and focus on the next event. The same was true if I did well: Savor it for a few minutes, remind myself of the things I did right, and then put it behind me so I could prepare for what was ahead.

Another way he helped to train me emotionally was by simulating meet conditions with what he called "ritual practices." He'd hand me the discus and say, "OK, you've got three throws and that's all." I couldn't take "just one more" until I felt good. That way I'd experience the pressure of a meet as well as learn to deal with the emotions of success or failure afterwards.

I truly enjoyed being on the team. Not only was I able to work hard, but I had a good time. Often during practices I'd back up my Pontiac to the track, open the trunk to expose a big pair of speakers, and blast my car stereo over the field. I found myself befriending my teammates and encouraging them in their events.

We had a good season as a team, placing second in the district. I was able to help significantly in the open competition and I did two decathlons. The first was the same meet in which I'd competed the previous year for Western Oregon State. Greg Hanson won again, scoring over 7000, but I improved to 6746 and took second place, setting a new school record. Coach Bakley's training and technical advice had given me the confidence I needed.

It felt great to be doing well, scoring lots of points for the team, and always improving. The whole season was that way—it got better and better. The more I worked on the decathlon, the more I began to understand why I enjoyed it so much. Certainly, I relished the challenge and the high scores, but I realized other things about it appealed to me. For one thing, it was an individual sport in which I had much more control than in most other sports. I worked out at my own pace and competed primarily against myself. There was no such thing as second or third string, and the coach couldn't take me out on a whim. I didn't have a long list of plays to memorize, no game films to watch each week, no mistakes by other team members that could hurt my performance. It was just me out there. I think this individuality aspect is what ultimately led me to drop my interest in football and concentrate on track.

I also discovered that the variety of events became a confidence-builder for me. Whether in practice or in a meet, something good would always happen. In a single-event competition, if you have a bad day, tough luck. There's no way to make up for it. But if I had a weak performance in the shot put, for example, I could turn around and have a great javelin throw and feel good about that. If I did poorly in a couple of events, I could compensate by doing better in others and still end up with a decent overall score.

Linn-Benton hosted the second decathlon in early May, which was a combined meet—the Oregon community college championship and the National Junior College Athletic Association (NJCAA) Region 18 championship. This was the big one, and I was psyched. Two days before the meet we had a very light workout in order to conserve energy. Coach Bakley walked up to me carrying a vaulting pole.

"Hey Dave," he said, "A coach friend of mine found this pole and asked me to check it out. It's new, but it doesn't have any markings on it. Would you be willing to take a run down the runway, plant it, and see if you can figure out what weight it might be?"

"Sure, no problem," I said. Coach Bakley had given me lots of help in the pole vault. He'd become a specialist in that event, and later two more of his athletes, Tim Bright and Kory Tarpenning, would go to the Olympics.

Maybe I ran too fast, or had too much energy built up for the meet, but as soon as I planted that pole it snapped like a pencil into three or four pieces. I took a nasty spill, just barely landing in the pit. Even worse, I fell on my right hand and dislocated my ring and middle fingers. Coach came running to help me up, wishing he'd never bothered with his friend's pole. I tried to shake it off and tell myself I'd be fine for the meet.

When I got up the morning of the meet, my whole hand was still swollen. Two of my fingers didn't work at all, and the others were sore. I could hardly grip anything. For the first time, I had to ask myself whether an injury would prevent me from competing. Should I forget about today's meet? I thought about it for maybe a minute.

No way.

I jumped in my car and buzzed over to campus. It was around eight o'clock, two hours before starting time. I parked at the very end of the lot, overlooking the track. The only people around were the guys setting up equipment and marking lines. For the next hour I sat there in the car with my stereo cranked up, surveying the field, flexing my sore hand, and getting myself pumped for the meet. I had made a tape of pop tunes that energized me for competition: "Jukebox Hero," and "I'm Gonna Win," by Foreigner, "The Runner Song," by Manfred Mann, and others. I called it my "moto tape." As the energy began to build inside me, so did the feeling that something big was going to come out of this decathlon.

When Coach Bakley asked how my hand was feeling, I said that it hurt, but I'd be fine. Without realizing it, I was following the advice he'd told us again and again in practice: Let go of the negatives, concentrate on the positives, and dismiss what you have no control over. I was determined to go out there and excel in this meet.

By the time the meet was over the next day, I had racked up 7225 points, placing first in the district and second in the region. I was exhilarated. That meet was the place I first believed I had a future in the decathlon. It wasn't just the high score, but how quickly I'd reached that score. I'd improved nearly a thousand points in just one year and three decathlons. My parents, who'd been watching the whole meet from the stands, came down and congratulated me. And Coach Bakley had a smile on his face that said, "I knew you could do it, Dave." Both he and I had the feeling that something special was happening. My only disappointment was that I would not be able to go to nationals, since LBCC teams no longer competed outside the region.

■ ■ ■

All spring I'd been trying to figure out what to do about the upcoming school year. I could still attend Linn-Benton, but I wouldn't be eligible for track, since I'd already competed two years at the community college level, so I started looking for another school. Coach Bakley had tried to get Oregon State College and the University of Oregon to recruit me, and I had talked to the coach at Oregon State, which was right in Corvallis. That would have been an ideal solution, I thought at the time. But neither school even returned the calls.

It just so happened that while the big regional meet was going on, Greg Hanson stopped to talk to me. He had beaten me the last two times we'd faced each other, and now I was returning the favor. We chatted a bit, and then he asked, "Where are you going to go to school next year?"

"Well, I'm not sure yet, maybe Oregon State or the University of Oregon."

"You should check into this school down in California— Azusa Pacific University," he said. "If I had to do it all over again, I would have gone there instead of Willamette."

"How come?"

He said he'd competed against several decathletes from there, and that they had a few other guys who were scoring in my range. In fact, the team had won the National Association of Intercollegiate Athletics (NAIA) nationals the year before. They seemed like good people to be around, and great people to train with. Then he said, "Anyway, you might want to think about it. It's a Christian school, but it's no big deal."

My ears perked up. A Christian school?

"Well, I'm a Christian," I said.

"Oh really? Hmm."

What a great idea. The perfect situation. A school with a championship track team, lots of decathletes as good as me or better, and, on top of it, a Christian atmosphere. Coach Bakley hadn't heard of it, but he encouraged me to check it out. So I found the number to Azusa Pacific, called them up, and asked for the track coach. His name was Terry Franson.

Our conversation was a little rushed, because he said he was busy preparing to go to nationals again. But his hoarse voice was friendly, and he seemed genuinely interested in me. When I told him my scores, he was impressed: there were only one or two guys at Azusa who had scored higher than my 7225. And my 203' javelin throw was at the national level in open competition. He asked me about the track season in Oregon, and how many months I was able to train. If I was scoring such good numbers in the raw, rainy climate of the Northwest, he thought, I'd do even better in Southern California with the warmer weather and a longer season.

Finally he said, "Dave, it's been good talking to you. I'm sorry I can't take any more time right now, but let me send you a packet of information about Azusa. Send me everything you've got on yourself, and then I'll call you back when we return from nationals, OK? Keep an eye on us there—we're going to do really well."

He also mentioned that Azusa Pacific was a Christian school, and that I could read all about it in the literature he was sending. As I hung up, I had a good feeling about this place.

I also felt good about the tremendously positive experience I'd had at Linn-Benton. I'd miss the friends I'd made on the team. To my surprise, they voted me "Most Inspirational" team member, something I'd never pictured myself receiving. Most of all, I'd miss Coach Bakley, who had been much more than a coach to me. He'd been my first mentor, someone who believed in me even before I believed in myself. He had brought stability and consistency to my athletic performance—and to some extent my life.

A week after talking with Coach Franson, a big envelope of information on the school arrived. And the following week I found the results of the NAIA national track and field competition in the newspaper. First place—Azusa Pacific

University. Barely a few more days had passed before the phone rang. It was Coach Franson.

"Dave, did you hear how it went at the NAIA Championships? We took first place!"

Obviously happy for the team, he told me how his athletes had fared in the various events. As it turned out, Doug Loisel of APU had placed first in the decathlon. I was more impressed by the minute: Not only had this Christian university won the nationals, but one of their athletes had won the decathlon. And his score was around 7500, only 300 points more than mine. We talked for a while longer, and when I mentioned that I needed financial help, he told me to send in all the forms and he'd see what he could do.

On my application I had listed Coach Bakley as a reference, so Coach Franson followed up and called him.

"Tell me about Dave," Franson said.

"He's an amazing athlete who hasn't even come close to reaching his potential," said Bakley. "And his attitude is such that his very presence will improve the performance of the entire team by fifteen to twenty-five points. Know what I mean?"

"Yeah—I know exactly what you mean. Now tell me, what kind of a citizen is he?"

"Well," Bakley said, "He's a little wild and crazy, but he's got a good heart and he's a good human being."

"That's all I need to know," said Franson.

I didn't hear the details of that conversation until much later, but as I reflect on it now, I wonder what would have happened if Coach Bakley had described me differently. He easily *could* have said, "Well, Dave drives like a maniac, gets drunk nearly every weekend, and has been arrested several times." It was true. Would Franson still have been interested in me?

In fact, one night only a week or two after my first phone call to Coach Franson, I had gotten drunk and wrecked my car. I'd gone to an end-of-the-year party at a friend's house and drank for most of the night. On the way home early the next morning, I swerved around on the wet roads just for the fun of it, and lost control of the car. Sliding sideways, I struck a line of ten mailboxes all perched on a horizontal two-by-four, and the long piece of wood crashed through the front windshield, grazed the top of the steering wheel, and rammed into the front seat next to me. Amazingly, I was unhurt except for a few scraped knuckles, which had been gripping the wheel as the wood passed over. There was no question in my mind that the two-by-four would have decapitated me it if had come through the side window.

When Coach Bakley talked with Coach Franson, he didn't know about *all* the trouble I'd gotten into, but he certainly knew I was a crazy driver and a big partier. And even though I'd never said anything to him about my young Christian faith, he somehow got a glimpse of the deeper part of me who wanted to be a better person and live purposefully.

Franson also learned from my application how I had become a Christian, and how I wanted to grow in my spiritual life. I fudged a little in the section on my church involvement, since I hadn't really been going to church, but I think they got the message that my commitment to Christ was real—even if it hadn't sunk in yet.

It was late June when I found out I'd been accepted at Azusa. The school offered me $2,000 in scholarship money for the year—which covered about one-fourth of my expenses. I needed more, but was grateful that they offered me something. I was psyched. And I appreciated the personal attention by the admissions department. Someone called with the names and numbers of others in my area who were also coming to APU, so I could make connections or combine for transportation. Those small touches made me feel comfortable and cared about. One name I recognized was Paul Webb, a hurdler I'd competed against from a nearby junior college. I phoned him and offered to give him a ride, since I was taking my car and needed help with gas money. We decided to be roommates.

Six weeks of summer remained before school, however. During the days I worked at a fiberglass factory near my dad's plant. It wasn't a bad job, except that I had to ride my bicycle back and forth because my car was waiting to be fixed. From time to time Dad would pop in and we'd have a Coke together. On the weekends, however, I kept up the drinking and partying with friends. I'd been doing it for so long now that I didn't know how to stop—even after it got me into trouble yet again.

It occurred one evening around the first of August. I was with my friend Jide, who now attended Oregon State right in Corvallis. We had been drinking and hanging out around the Oregon State campus, which was completely closed down for the summer, and, just for fun, we decided to climb on top of one of the fifteen-story dormitories to see what it was like on the roof. Pretty nice view, actually, until we spotted the campus security cars coming. We tried to hurry down and run, but they caught us and turned us over to the city police.

Again we were accused of trying to break in, but this time we received more than a slap on the wrist. They fingerprinted us, took our mug shots, even conducted a humiliating strip search. At that I broke down and cried. I couldn't believe they were doing this to us just for goofing off. But there was more: They then proceeded to toss us in jail. Jide and I had to spend the night in a five-by-eight-foot pen with nothing but an open toilet and a bed.

As I sat there in that cell, a million thoughts raced through my head. *I can't believe this is happening. I'm a Christian who's going to a Christian university in a couple of weeks, and here I am sitting in jail! What if the school finds out and decides not to let me in? What if I have to stay in jail? What if my parents find out? Why did I do such a stupid thing? I'm supposed to be changing my life now that I'm a Christian.*

Around noon the next day we stood before a judge. He glanced over the paperwork, then looked at us.

"You guys spent the night in jail?" he asked. "For this?"

I sighed in relief. At least I wasn't the only one who thought it was a bit harsh.

"You guys have paid for your crime," he said. "This case is dismissed—you are free to go."

Believe me—we went. Fast. I was so ashamed that I didn't tell Mom and Dad about it until years later.

I can't say that my night in jail brought about a profound change or suddenly revitalized my spiritual life. But as strange as it sounds, I did have an inner sense that Jesus was present, and that this was happening to me for a reason. Maybe he realized I needed a wake-up call from the police in order to start pulling my life together. I felt sorry for flubbing up so badly, and I believe God forgave me. *I'm gonna be OK,* I told myself afterwards. *I still have a lot of potential to make something of my life.*

A few days before I left for Azusa, I went out in the back yard where Dad was weeding the flowers. "Well, Dad, I'm gonna be gone soon, and I'm gonna miss you and Mom," I said. "But I want you to know this is a major step for me—it's like the beginning of my life. I'm becoming a man now, and I'm gonna be somebody by going where I'm going."

I wanted to remind him that this was a positive move for me, that he should feel good about it. Maybe I was reminding myself, too, because I was scared.

Dad looked up from the flower bed, and I saw tears in his eyes. He never talked a lot, but he's always been a sensitive man, as well as a hard worker. I'm sure all sorts of things were flowing through his mind as we stood there. His son Dave was finally going off on his own—too far away to pop home for the weekend. Dave, with all that energy and athletic ability, but also with a knack for getting into trouble. I'll never know all that he felt at that moment, but in the quiet I knew he understood.

All he said was that he was proud of me, and excited that I had this great opportunity. If I ever needed him, he would be there.

Since I was leaving early in the morning, Mom made a big goodbye dinner the night before and some of my friends joined us—Amit, Jide, and several others. I felt a little of the same sadness I had when I left Missoula—sadness that things would never be the same again. This time, however, I had a much greater sense of anticipation for what awaited me. I was scared, but at least I had chosen this new direction. I could accept it more easily. True, things would never be the same. Instead, they'd be *better*.

"I love you—I'll see you for Christmas," I told Mom and Dad the next morning, giving them both a big hug. Then I picked up Paul, and the two of us took off for Southern California.

400 meters

PR: 48.19

It's the last event of the first day. If you're at a big meet, it's probably dark outside. As you get into the blocks, you're saying to yourself, "I'm sick of this decathlon—I want to go home." Your job is to figure out a way to use that feeling to your advantage. My approach is to picture this event as one long scream—a sustained, fifty-second release of energy, frustration, anger, and pain.

The 400 is an all-out sprint for one lap around the track. The hardest part is dealing with the anxiety of knowing the last fifty to one hundred meters will be incredibly painful. You know it's going to hurt before you start; there's no way around it. But since the pain will only last for a while, you know you can survive. For me, it's a real rush to do the 400. The challenge of finishing fast in spite of the pain makes it exciting.

As the race begins, you go all out and try to get ahead as fast as you can, as if you were running the 100 meters. But you can only run that hard for thirty to fifty meters before you have to take something off your pace. You'd die if you ran that fast for the entire lap. For the next 250 meters, you need to establish a rhythm that gives you good speed but still allows you to conserve some energy for the finish. If you use too much energy at the beginning, you'll be completely spent before the end and you'll finish with a pathetic time.

Between 200 and 300 meters, your oxygen stores begin to run out and your muscles scream back at you to slow down. It feels as if a fifty-pound weight has jumped on your back. Your whole body wants to quit. Somehow you have to control your mind's reaction to the pain and press on as fast as you can. Finally, when you have eighty to a hundred meters left and the pain has really set in, you release that last reserve of energy you've been holding onto and kick hard for a strong finish.

As painful and as consuming as it is, the 400 has taught me about the challenge of facing adversity. It has shown me that I can learn from my problems or difficulties if I don't shy away from the pain they're going to produce in me. No one likes pain—the physical or the emotional kind. But if you expect it, plan for it, and learn to go through it rather than avoid it, you'll be a stronger person when the race is over.

■ ■ ■

▪ chapter six ▪

NO LIMITS

THE LAST FORTY-FIVE minutes to Azusa on the 210 Freeway seemed like three hours. I was so excited about this school that I couldn't wait to get there. Seeing all the lights and the urban sprawl only added to my excitement. I knew I was driving not just to another college, but to my future.

Paul and I had talked and joked for most of the sixteen-hour drive. We had plenty in common since we came from the same area, played the same sport, even went to some of the same meets. And on top of it, we were both Christians and now roommates at Azusa Pacific University.

We pulled into the parking lot sometime after ten at night, unsure of what to do or where to stay. Even at that late hour, the school had people there who showed us where to check in and get our room key. I felt comfortable right away, and enjoyed getting settled during the next week before classes began. Other than the smog, which I only noticed for a few days, the place felt like home. To my surprise, the campus actually looked as beautiful as it did in the promotional materials they'd sent me.

I met Coach Terry Franson during registration several days later. Paul pointed him out to me, and I nervously walked over to introduce myself. He was busy helping several students with their class schedules. He had a kind, friendly face, and looked younger than I had expected. As I came up to him,

I felt shy and afraid, maybe even a little paranoid about making a good first impression.

"Hi, Coach Franson—I'm Dave Johnson." So far so good.

"Hey, Dave—nice to finally meet you," he said warmly. "I'm glad that you're here."

In my excitement, I blurted out the next thing that popped into my head:

"You look bigger than I thought you would be."

Not exactly a compliment, but not really an insult either. Actually, I wasn't even thinking about his size—I only said it out of nervousness. I might have gotten away with it, too, except Paul had said the exact same words to him just the day before. I felt like a real geek. Coach handled it fine, however, smiling and shaking my hand before returning to his registration duties. I was able to laugh it off afterwards.

Everything I encountered at APU was new and exciting— my courses, the small classes, the relaxed environment, and the teachers who not only knew their subject material, but wanted to be my friend as well. A family atmosphere prevailed. There were still times that I felt self-conscious and afraid, such as in communications class when I had to stand up and give my own speech. I was so nervous that I read it straight off the paper. But overall I felt my social confidence improving.

Azusa Pacific was the first school I'd attended where the professors prayed before class and showed how the various academic disciplines related to Christianity. It was especially meaningful in my psychology class since I'd declared a psych major. I realized that everything I was learning was part of the vast knowledge God had given to the world, and that the purpose of my education was to assimilate this truth in order to serve Christ better.

Another new experience was required chapel every Monday, Wednesday, and Friday for an hour. Some students found chapel boring or unnecessary since they were already involved in churches. But because I'd never been consistent about going to church since I quit going with my parents, I went with a different mindset, and actually enjoyed it. I liked being able to focus on God, sing songs, and hear teaching from Scripture so consistently.

The school did have one problem, however: a list of strict rules. Well, they seemed pretty strict to me, at least: no drinking or smoking on campus, separate dorms for men and women, and no members of the opposite sex allowed in our rooms except for a few hours one evening a week. Two of my traditionally favorite activities—drinking and womanizing—were severely curtailed. I went crazy on weekends, because I wanted to drink and party like I'd always done. But I wasn't legal drinking age and I didn't know anybody who I could ask to get beer for me. It suddenly hit me that I was very sheltered in this place.

The rules made me mad at first. *I'm paying for this school*, I said to myself. *I should be able to do what I want*. But then I began to compare it to the other two schools I'd attended. At Western Oregon State there was always a party to go to; several days a week I was staying out half the night, and my classwork had suffered. My life had had very little structure or direction. During my time at Linn-Benton I lived at home, caught between the party life and the handful of Christian friends I'd made. Virtually every time I got into trouble I'd been drinking.

At Azusa, however, I wasn't caught between two worlds; I was part of an environment that embodied Christian values. Perhaps the rules here weren't arbitrary restrictions after all, but a way of helping me to channel my energy in positive directions. I thought about all the negative things I'd done over the years—drinking, smoking marijuana, troublemaking, fooling around with women. They were fun at times, certainly, but they sidetracked me from the kind of life I really wanted—a life of purpose, a life that would make a difference in the world. Not to mention the life that *God* wanted for me. Could it be that Azusa's limits on negative behavior might actually *increase* my ability to change in positive ways?

As the school year progressed, I began to see the wisdom behind the rules. They helped me to focus on what was most important: growing in every area of my life—physically, intellectually, emotionally, and spiritually. It may not have been the case for everyone, but I knew I *needed* the "sheltering" APU provided in order to become a stronger person. I felt myself changing and adopting positive values that would make the world a better place.

Meanwhile, Coach Franson called the track team together in October to begin practicing for the indoor season, which ran from December through February. Three times a week we'd begin practice with a team meeting, where Coach Franson would say a few words and then we'd all pray together. It felt very awkward at first, because I wasn't used to holding someone's hand and praying out loud. I *wanted* to pray, even knew what I wanted to say, but I felt self-conscious.

Once I got used to it, however, I found myself looking forward to those meetings. They helped us gain the proper perspective *before* working out. Then, when we began practice, we knew our purpose in being there was not to stroke our egos, not to glorify Azusa Pacific, not to win for its own sake, but to be representatives of Christ on the athletic field. That meant striving to do our absolute best with the abilities he gave us.

Coach Franson was like a father figure to me. He cared about me and the other team members in a personal way, and like Coach Bakley, he tried to nurture the whole person. He certainly wanted me to be a great athlete, but more than that he wanted me to be a great person, a "warrior for Christ," as he would say. He stressed that our team was a Christ-centered team, and that we needed to reflect Christ at all times—not only in our performance, but in our relationships with each other, on and off the track. If we weren't giving one hundred percent of our athletic ability, or if we harbored resentment toward a teammate or complained behind his back, we weren't reflecting Christ. He told us to affirm and encourage each other, and to resolve our differences quickly or ask his help. As a result, he created a positive and supportive team atmosphere.

And that kind of atmosphere inspired me to train hard. Our workouts took place on Azusa's "hillside campus," a five-minute ride up into the foothills of the San Gabriel Mountains.

Some found it inconvenient to drive to the gym and the track, but I liked getting away from the noise and traffic of the downtown area. Twice a week Coach would send us all running up and down a steep fire road, and I pumped myself into top shape on that hill. The seclusion, the quiet, and the panoramic view all made for one great place to work out.

It may sound like I immediately understood everything that was happening to me at Azusa and exactly how I was changing. No way. I didn't realize many of these things until much later. At the time, I felt more like a blank sheet of paper, one that had been partially crumpled. I knew I needed the wrinkles ironed out, though, and I had the feeling that my experience at this school would somehow fill the lines on the paper with extremely valuable insights. I had an intense desire to learn everything I could, to squeeze every drop of meaning from each experience and use it in a positive way. And, gradually, changes started taking place.

When I went home for Christmas break, I noticed a few small changes. I felt more comfortable, more adult around my parents, and found it easier to communicate with them. I set a goal to get to know them better. I enjoyed seeing my friends Jide and Jim, and even drank with them a few times, but I handled it differently. Instead of getting rip-roaring drunk, I'd say to myself, *That's enough, Dave—you've reached your limit,* and grab a soda instead. It felt good to be able to associate with my old friends while also setting healthy limits.

Back at school, I did some serious training for my first APU decathlon, scheduled for late January. It was an outdoor meet at Cal State-LA, and decathletes from big schools such as UCLA and USC would be there, as well as older post-collegiate decathletes. I'd watched a decathlon in December at Long Beach State, and now I was ready to compete.

It must have been all the things I'd been learning and experiencing during the fall. I'd finally begun to understand my purpose in life, and I was so excited, so motivated that I charged onto the track and took first place in collegiate competition and second overall. My score was 7570, nearly 350 points better than my last decathlon at Linn-Benton, and a new school record at APU.

What a great feeling—to get a big score in my first meet as an APU Cougar. Coach Franson was surprised to see such rapid improvement, although he chalked some of it up to the warmer training weather. Even more surprised were the other decathletes on the team (six or seven in all), several of whom had been wondering whether I'd *really* scored 7225 at Linn-Benton. After all, I was the new guy and they'd never seen me compete. That first meet pretty much put their questions to rest.

At the same time, however, it raised a new question for me. This was 1984, an Olympic year, and the Games were to be held right here in Los Angeles. The overall winner of the meet had qualified for the Olympic Trials with a score of 7780—only 210 points more than I'd scored. Could I reach the qualifying score of 7625 in time for the Olympic Trials?

I'd never even *thought* about the Olympic Games before; I hardly knew what they were. But after that meet in January it seemed that I kept hearing about the Olympics wherever I went. My curiosity was aroused. I started reading about some of the great decathletes of recent years such as Bruce Jenner and Daley Thompson. And in my workouts I felt like I had so much more energy yet to unleash. The Olympic Games. That's what I wanted to go for. I'd never even seen them on TV before, but I knew I wanted to be there. My main goal for the year, I decided, would be to compete at the Olympic Trials.

A few weeks later, I shared my goal with Coach Franson. Each year he asks everybody on the team to write down their track and field goals in several areas—team goals, individual goals, Christian goals, and any other goals. Under team goals I talked about our need for unity, and expressed hope that we would catch other people's attention by our faith and our dedication to the sport. Under spiritual goals, I said that I wanted Christ to be at the center of my athletic performance, and that I wanted my performance—win or lose—to point to Christ's presence in my life. Individually, I wrote that I wanted to give one hundred percent and reach the highest level of achievement that my gifts would allow. I put down distances, times, and heights that I wanted to attain for each event. Then I added two more items: I wanted to go to the Olympic Trials, and I wanted to score 8000 points.

Actually, my list of goals was not nearly as detailed as many of the others. Most of the decathletes on the team carried around a little book with scoring tables for each event in the decathlon, and reported exact point totals on their sheet. I never used the book, and never really kept track of my performance that way. Occasionally, Coach Franson photocopied a few pages for me to use, and I'd end up losing them. All I knew is that I wanted my overall score to be better than the last time, or my scores in each event to be better than my highest score so far. Of course, I needed to be aware of point values, but it felt too limiting to keep them with me all the time. If I'd focused too much on how many additional points I could have eked out of each event, I probably would never have set 8000 as a goal. Or believed I could reach it.

Coach sat down with me in his office a few days later. He was holding my goal sheet in his hand. He affirmed my team and spiritual goals, and went over some of my individual numbers with me. Then he paused for a moment.

"Dave, we need to talk about this 8000," he said. "You need to be careful—8000 points is a big jump from your present PR." He wasn't trying to talk me out of my goal. Instead, like any good coach, he was gently suggesting that I might be trying to achieve more than I was capable of in my first year at APU. He wanted us to set high goals, but he also wanted to prepare us for not reaching them, just in case.

"But Coach, I think I can do it, I really do," I said. "I'll be able to score enough to go to the Trials, and then at the Trials I think I can score 8000 points."

I know he wanted to believe me, but it was still a big leap from 7570 to 8000. His face remained somewhat skeptical.

"I really think I have that kind of score in me," I pressed. "I can do it, if you'll help me."

The truth is, I knew I couldn't do it on my own. And even with help, it wouldn't be easy. I'd definitely need Coach Franson's expertise and support—which I was already getting. But even more than that, I'd need Jesus Christ to help me. If I was to accomplish anything, it would have to be for him.

"Well OK," Coach said, remaining cautious. "It's good to have that high of a goal, but just be prepared in case you don't make it. I'll do everything I can to help." He kept a positive tone, but I think he didn't endorse it wholeheartedly because he wanted to be available to listen and support me if I had trouble getting there.

Training continued into the spring outdoor track season. Even in January and February the temperatures were moderate enough for us to practice outdoors. I liked having the extra workout months, and I felt myself getting stronger in each event. I was pleased with my 7570 in that first decathlon, but I knew I was capable of doing much better. Good things were going to happen; I could feel it. My training with Coach Franson was moving forward. He introduced me to Mike Barnett, an APU alum and U.S. champion in the javelin, to help me in that event. And help me he did—my distance improved nearly forty feet, from 204 to 241 feet. In addition, the team was having a winning season, and I contributed in several of the open events—hurdles, pole vault, javelin, and mile relay.

My next decathlon took place in March at Occidental College in Eagle Rock. I was hoping to do well there and qualify for the Trials, but a few minor things went wrong and threw off my concentration. I scored 7546—twenty-four points less than my previous meet. Certainly a respectable score, but disappointing to me, because it was the first decathlon in which I hadn't improved over the previous one. It felt like a setback. Up to this point I'd been carrying around the illusion that I would keep improving with every decathlon. Now my perfect plan had suddenly been rocked. *I can't believe I didn't improve,* I fretted. *I set a goal and didn't reach it. I didn't achieve what I thought I could do. Maybe I've been fantasizing, and it's not really going to happen.*

Coach Franson helped me sort through my feelings. Through him I learned one of many important lessons about track and about life: that I didn't have to be the "perfect" decathlete who always scored more points than the last time. No athlete in any sport has ever improved his score in every single performance. Everyone has good days and bad days, he said, and most college decathletes would die to reach my "bad" score of 7546 on a *good* day. Maybe I needed to relax a little, accept that I was a fallible human being, and try to learn from whatever mistakes I'd made. He didn't tell me to abandon my goals—just to remember that I wouldn't necessarily reach them immediately. As in anything, there was a growth process involved that took time. That lesson helped me to be more realistic as an athlete without losing my drive to achieve. It made me stronger. Over the next month, I trained harder, but worried less about constantly reaching higher scores.

There were two significant meets in April, both in the same week. First was the California Invitational, sponsored by Azusa Pacific, which consisted only of the decathlon for men and the heptathlon for women. Since APU didn't have a very good track at that time—only a dirt track up on the hill—we ran our meet at Cal Poly in Pomona. Cal Poly also happened to be located right next to Mt. San Antonio College, the site of the second major event, the Mt. SAC Relays—Southern California's biggest track meet and its most important decathlon.

Mt. SAC is something of a big-name meet in which many athletes come to compete in only one or two events. Carl Lewis, Edwin Moses, Roger Kingdom, Evelyn Ashford, Florence Griffith-Joyner, and Jackie Joyner-Kersee might all make appearances. College athletes could also participate if they reach qualifying scores in a particular event. Our team would compete in most events, including the shuttle hurdles (for which I ran anchor), but I hadn't yet reached the qualifying score of 7625 to compete in the decathlon. So I remained content to do APU's California Invitational Decathlon.

Because there were no individual events—only a decathlon and a heptathlon—the meet moved along at a good clip. Even with thirty decathletes participating, we never had to wait more than a half-hour between events, so we finished each of the two days in five or six hours. I was more relaxed than usual, probably because I'd taken some of the pressure off myself to be superhuman. I had finally realized I didn't need to be invincible; I could just go out there, give it my very best, and trust God with the results.

The attitude adjustment worked: I had an incredible meet. On the first day I set personal records in three events—100, long jump, and high jump—and a PR for my first day total. The second day went even better, with PRs in the hurdles, pole vault, and javelin. My final score? 8043 points. Barely two months after writing down my goals, I'd suddenly reached both of them in one fell swoop. I'd qualified for the Olympic Trials, and I'd passed the 8000 mark.

The high score blew me away. A typical decathlete, if there is such a thing, might score 5900 or 6000 in his first meet. By his tenth decathlon, he may be in the 7500 to 7800 range. This was only the sixth decathlon of my life, and I'd scored over 8000. I had honestly believed I'd reach 8000 at *some* point, but not right away. I thought I'd qualify for the Trials and then perhaps be charged up enough to score 8000 there. News of the meet hit the sports page the next day. This twenty-one-year-old kid no one had ever heard of had just qualified for the Olympic Trials, and his score was high enough to make him a serious contender for the Olympic team. At that time, the top decathlete in the United States had scored 8200 points, and the second-best score was around 8100. I was amazed to discover I had come that close to the best in the country.

That incredible week still hadn't ended. A day later I ran the shuttle hurdles (an exhibition event) for APU at the Mt. SAC Relays. In the shuttle hurdles, a team runs the 110-meter high hurdles four times, one runner for each stretch. The guys on our team were Doug Loisel, Brian Arnold, my roommate Paul Webb, and me. Energized by my decathlon performance,

I ran a 13.9 split—my best ever—and we won first place. Afterwards, other coaches kept coming up to Franson saying, "Who is this Dave Johnson guy? He scores over 8000 yesterday in the decathlon, and then today he runs a 13.9 hurdles!" I hadn't noticed, but Coach Franson told me that all during the meet, people in the Mt. SAC stadium were buzzing about Dave Johnson's performance. And to top it all off, the winning score of their decathlon was 8150 by Mike Ramos of Washington State—just a hundred points ahead of me.

Coach Franson was one proud papa. He was more amazed than I was. I think something changed in both of us after that week. My respect and trust in him deepened significantly, because he had put me in touch with my life-purpose, Christ, the One who inspired me to excel. Coach had also supported me in reaching my goals in spite of his doubts. My self-confidence grew, and I began to think that with Christ at the center of my life, there might be no limit to what I could achieve.

What changed in him, I think, was that he came to believe more strongly that he was on track in his approach to coaching. He began to expect more from athletes who wanted to go all out for Christ, even if their faith had lots of rough edges, like mine did. Without becoming unrealistic, he grew a little less cautious. From then on, whenever I came up with an idea or set a goal, he'd nod and say, "OK, let's go for it and see what happens."

The other decathletes on the APU team gave me hearty congratulations. One guy, Tim Payne, took me out for a steak dinner. We'd been friends and training companions throughout the year.

"Dave, I can't believe you scored that high," he said as we ate. "That makes you one of the best decathletes in the history of the United States." I'd never thought of it that way before.

Another teammate, Shane Paynor, said, "Dave, each time you step out on the track now, people around you are gonna say, 'Hey—there's Dave Johnson, the decathlete.'" I'd never really thought about that before either.

In fact, the whole idea of being known by the public for my accomplishments hadn't occurred to me. I had just wanted to find out how far I could go by giving one hundred percent and doing it for the Lord. Reaching my goals told me that God was with me, and that he wanted to use the decathlon as part of his will for my life. After all, I was a young Christian and a young decathlete. As I grew more mature spiritually, mentally, and physically, I wondered, who knew what might happen?

The Olympic Trials were to take place in June. But first we had the NAIA nationals in Charleston, West Virginia. Coach and I decided to pass on the decathlon at the nationals in order to save myself for the Trials. I'd throw the javelin, do the hurdles, and run the mile relay. Looking back, that might have been a mistake.

I was nervous and excited on the plane trip to West Virginia. Not only had I never competed in a national meet, but I'd never flown in a commercial airplane before. I surrounded myself with air sickness bags, and kept my face pressed to the window like a wide-eyed kid. To feel the huge aircraft take off was awesome, and I remember thinking, *Man, look what the Lord's providing in my life. Who knows where I would have ended up without him? Now here I am on this airplane traveling at 500 miles an hour to be in a national track meet. And all my teammates from Azusa Pacific are here with me.*

For the second year in a row, APU won the NAIA national championships. Last year at this time I'd read about it in the back of the *Oregonian* sports section. This year, I personally contributed to that championship. I took second place in the javelin with a throw of 239 feet. My other two events didn't go as well: I tripped over a hurdle and didn't make it to the finals in that event, and our mile relay team was disqualified because one of the guys stepped on the lane line. But it still felt great to win the nationals. Our decathletes did well, too: Doug Loisel, the former school record holder, won the decathlon for the second straight year with a score of 7623. I was happy for him, except that he narrowly missed qualifying for the Olympic Trials—a goal he'd been shooting for.

Only a few weeks later, I'd have to face disappointment myself at the Los Angeles Coliseum, where the Olympic Trials were held. Even after much preparation and training, I only managed a score of 7670, good for eleventh place out of fifty-four decathletes. I didn't bomb in any of the events, but I didn't outdo myself either. This had been the biggest meet of my life—the first with a large crowd, major media coverage, and twice as many decathletes as I'd ever seen in one place. At the time I couldn't figure out what my problem was. I knew I was capable of winning a spot on the Olympic team, and I'd been trusting God for strength. What had happened?

Looking back, I'd sum up the situation in four words: too much, too soon. This was only my seventh decathlon ever, and my very first at the national level. I hadn't had enough experience yet to feel relaxed and compete effectively in a big meet. Up to that point, my biggest meet had been the NAIA nationals a few weeks back, and I hadn't even done the decathlon there. Perhaps if I had, I would have been a little better prepared, but probably not by much.

In one short year, I had gone from a small meet at an Oregon community college to one of the largest and most important meets in the country; from competing before a handful of family members to facing thousands of spectators in the Coliseum. I didn't know how to handle the pressure yet, and hadn't learned to focus on the task before me without getting caught up in all the hoopla.

I needed more time. And more experience.

I probably should have said to myself, *Not bad—eleventh place in my first Olympic Trials,* and then let it go. Instead, I was mad that I didn't make the team—half mad at God, and half mad at myself. This had been my big chance, I thought, and now that chance was gone.

It took most of the summer for me to get over it. But after a few visits to bars and a few episodes of drinking, I woke up and realized I didn't want to return to my old ways. As I prepared for the coming school year, I vowed to begin training hard for 1988.

110-meter hurdles

PR: 14.17

Twelve hours ago you were running as if there was no tomorrow. You wake up stiff and sore only to realize that it came after all.

First thing, you have to go back out on the track and race for 110 meters at top speed while jumping over ten 42-inch barriers. You're not even awake yet, and you're faced with ten different chances to trip and break your neck. Try it sometime.

But the first challenge of the hurdles occurs even before you start as you try to loosen up your stiff, tired body. I always try to pretend that this is the first day and the first event of competition. Anything to get me thinking positively about this third-most-difficult event of the decathlon.

The technical difficulty of the hurdles arises mostly because they require repetition, rhythm, and balance. If any of these is upset, it slows you down and effectively lowers your points. There is no penalty for hitting a hurdle—if it didn't slow you down so much, you could steamroll right through all ten of them. The point of the event is not *whether* you can get past all the hurdles, but *how efficiently* you can do it.

When the gun goes off, you cross the first hurdle and get into a rhythm—1-2-3-kick, 1-2-3-kick. You feel like a thoroughbred jumping horse. You hit that stride—it's called "three-stepping"—and you fly.

But sometimes things happen, and you have to be prepared. If you graze one of the hurdles you're not penalized, but your rhythm and balance are thrown off a little and you have to adjust. And there's always some fear that you'll catch a hurdle and fall down. You can hit as many hurdles as you want, but if one of them takes you down you probably won't finish the race—plus, you can get hurt. That doesn't happen frequently, but it's a real possibility.

When I blow out of the blocks, I try to take an aggressive approach to the hurdles. It's either them or me. If I don't clear them, I'm going to deliver them a blow rather than let them grab me and bring me down. So I count 1–2–3 and then kick at each hurdle. If I hit it, that hurdle is going to fall over and I'm going to keep running. It's not a very delicate approach, but it works for me. So far I haven't knocked over many hurdles, and I haven't gone down.

I sometimes think of the hurdles as a little picture of the decathlon—ten hurdles, ten events. Even more, the hurdles can represent life, which never gives us one test that we pass or fail, but instead presents us with a series of obstacles to overcome as we reach toward our goals. If we stay focused on that goal and maintain a healthy rhythm and balance in the way we live, we'll meet those challenges with the least difficulty. Sometimes an individual hurdle may seem like a mountain, and we may trip over it, but it's only one hurdle. It doesn't have to take us off course. Neither the hurdles nor life require perfection of us. We can recover and move on until we've accomplished what we set out to do.

■　■　■

chapter seven

QUEST FOR THE BEST

IN SPITE OF MY disappointment over the Olympic Trials, I reminded myself that my first year at Azusa Pacific University had been a time of incredible growth and discovery. In only nine short months, it had affected virtually every area of my life. Well, every area except one: my love life.

Most of the summer of 1984 I stayed in Azusa, working for the college as a janitor (along with future Kansas City Chiefs football star Christian Okoye), and several nights a week as a security guard off campus. I shared a campus apartment with three other athletes, and we enjoyed hanging out and clowning around together. At one point I told my roommates, Nate Oliverson, Tim Lomheim, and Cres Gonzales, that I was primed to find my future wife during this next school year. I even predicted she would be blond and blue-eyed.

Sure enough, that fall it happened. Nate and I had missed dinner in the cafeteria because we'd shown up late. Outside the cafeteria door we noticed two striking freshman coeds in the same predicament. Feeling studly and chivalrous, we seized the opportunity and offered to take them out to dinner. The girls' names were Bobby Baine and Sheri Jordan, and they were both blond. When we arrived at the restaurant in a borrowed car (I'd sold my own because I needed money), Nate and I stepped aside and tried to figure out who would sit with

who. Neither of us had a strong preference for one girl over the
other, so we devised a plan: I would go to the men's room
while Nate sat down in the booth, and presumably the girl
interested in Nate would sit on his side. Problem solved.

   To my dismay, when I returned from the men's room,
Nate was sitting all by himself on one side with a funny look
on his face. Both girls were sitting across from him. We ended
up having a lot of fun, though. I liked both of them, but leaned
slightly toward pursuing Bobby. What's weird is that I never
asked her out, though I would always say hi to Sheri when I
saw her. Eventually, I started teasing Sheri about when she was
going to return the dinner favor, until one night she agreed to
take me out for a frozen yogurt. We had a good time, and I
learned that she came from the town of Sweet Home, Oregon,
just forty-five minutes from Corvallis.

   Thus began our dating relationship, which had many fun
and zany moments. One of the things we liked to do together
was play video games in the Student Center late at night.
(Since I was a janitor, I had access to the building after it
closed.) We didn't have much money, but we soon found that
by taping a string onto a quarter we could play for hours.

   I enjoyed being with Sheri, but I also wanted to goof off
with my buddies sometimes. One Saturday I was eating in the
cafeteria with the guys, planning some fun for the night, when,
out of the corner of my eye I saw Sheri approaching from the
other side of the room. I knew that if I acknowledged her and
told her what we were planning, she'd either want to come
along or do something else alone with me, so I decided to pretend I didn't see her coming. Quickly, I hopped up from my
chair and hustled toward the door. To add a little dazzle to my
exit, and perhaps distract Sheri from thinking I was avoiding
her, I hurdled over two of the tables. Fortunately, she found it
funny, and I still had my night out with the guys.

   Sheri and I would continue dating for the next three years.
The more time I spent with her, the more things I liked. I
admired her strong Christian faith, and the seriousness with
which she took her studies. She had lots of energy, worked

hard at whatever she did, and had set high goals for her nursing career. She was in the APU choir, and I loved going to hear her sing in their concerts. And on top of it, she was one beautiful woman. Back in Oregon she'd even won a Modern Miss pageant. We would have plenty of time to get to know each other. After all, she was only a freshman, and I was a second-semester junior still trying to figure out my life.

This would also be my last year of eligibility for track, since I'd competed two years in Oregon and one here at Azusa. So I had some decisions to make about my future. I had received a generous scholarship offer from UCLA after last year's season, but I didn't want to leave Azusa's supportive environment. I thought about "redshirting," which would allow me to train with the team but not compete, thus extending my eligibility another year. That way I could retain my scholarship, focus on my courses, and perhaps get my senior year of school paid for.

Coach Franson advised against redshirting because the team needed me too much for points. But he did push the school for more financial help for me since I'd had such a good previous year in track. I was awarded slightly more than a half-scholarship, which eased my monetary worries somewhat.

■ ■ ■

After three straight years of dramatic improvement in the decathlon, in 1985 I finally had what I'd call an average year. I did four decathlons, and never passed the 8000 mark—although I got close once or twice. I felt like I was improving in my events, but I just wasn't getting the additional points. At the Fresno State Decathlon in April, I took first place with a score of 7948. But soon after that I strained a tendon in my right elbow, which affected my javelin throwing. It would bother me for an entire year, though I was still able to compete. To further complicate matters, a new javelin had been introduced that year which did not fly as far as the old one, and I found it difficult to adjust.

In May we went to the NAIA nationals in Hillsdale, Michigan. This time I would do the decathlon there, and I was favored to win. My first day of competition went very well; I was leading the pack at the end of the day, had PR'd in the long jump and shot put, and came close to my PRs in the other events. If I continued at this pace, I'd end up with a total of 8100, breaking the NAIA nationals record by 500 points. This would be the big victory, the big breakthrough I needed.

On the second day I got good points in the hurdles and discus. But then something went wrong with the pole vault. It was one of my weaker events at this point, and I hadn't trained for it well enough during the year. Still, I figured I'd have no trouble clearing my opening height of twelve feet. Unfortunately, I couldn't get my approach down, and there was confusion between me and the assistant by the runway who was supposed to help me gauge my steps accurately. My second and third attempts were worse than the first.

I was crushed. Here I was, the odds-on favorite to win the nationals, and I had just no-heighted in the pole vault. My score for that event, zero, made it virtually impossible to win. I was sad and upset—I'd let myself down, I'd let my coach down, I'd let my team down. I wanted to quit the meet. But Coach Franson urged me to finish out the last two events, the javelin and the 1500 meters. "You never know," he said, "you might still be able to win."

My final score was only 7255, a pretty unimpressive total. But Coach reminded me afterwards that while 7255 may be an ordinary score for *ten* events, it was an excellent score for *nine* events. I'd done so well in nine that I beat every decathlete present except one—the winner—who had scored 7540. That brought some comfort, even if it didn't bring me the championship.

My next meet was the TAC National Championships in Indianapolis, equal to the Olympic Trials in significance and held in June during the three non-Olympic years. (TAC stands for The Athletics Congress, the national governing body for track and field in the U.S., which changed its name to USA

Giving it all I've got during the Mt. SAC Relays at APU in the spring of 1991.

A

B

C

Sheri and I have truly been blessed with the addition of Alexandra to our family.

Left page

A. At nine months old, I was already full of energy.

Background and B. Although I was never too interested in sports, they seemed to come naturally to me. Baseball and bowling gave me my first taste of what it was like to be the best.

C. Dressed for church, I pose with my brother and sisters. From left: Me, Gary, Barbara, and Cathy.

Right page

Background: I spent my senior year at Crescent Valley High after moving with my family to Corvallis, Oregon.

A. Our 1988 family Christmas photo. Clockwise from left: Gary, Cathy, Barbara, me, Dad, Lois, and Mom.

A

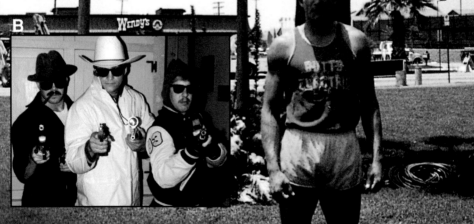

Sheri and I left the church with my vaulting poles tied to the side of the car.

Left page

A. The APU track team in the spring of 1985—my last year of collegiate competition.

Background: APU congratulated me after I won my first National Championship in Eugene, Oregon, in June, 1986.

B. My years at Azusa bring back some fun memories. Here, Ron Buck, Mike Rutherford, and I find time to clown around.

C. Ron Buck (left), Nate Oliverson (right), and I pose on our motorcycles in front of newly renamed Bike Hall.

Right page

Background: After three years of dating, Sheri and I married on June 12, 1987.

A. We called Sheri's car "The Shark" because of its pointed front end.

A

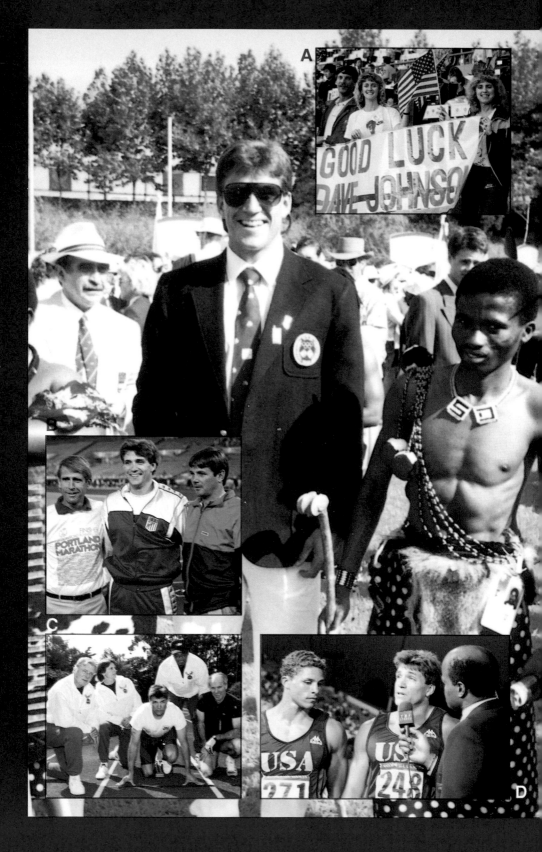

A

GOOD LUCK
DAVE JOHNSON

B

PORTLAND MARATHON

C

USA
271

USA
248

D

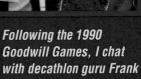

Following the 1990 Goodwill Games, I chat with decathlon guru Frank Zarnowski.

Left page

Background: My first Olympic experience was Seoul in 1988. I really enjoyed the opening ceremonies.

A. Some of my greatest fans came to cheer me on.

B. I wouldn't have made it to the Olympics without the encouragement of Coaches Bakley and Franson.

C. At the first VISA decathlon camp in 1990. I'm with former gold medalists Bob Mathias, Bruce Jenner, Milt Campbell, and Bill Toomey.

D. Dan O'Brien and I are interviewed by TBS Sports after the Goodwill Games.

Right page

Background: A victory lap after winning the Goodwill Games.

A. The discus is a highly technical event. Here I'm competing at the Mt. SAC Relays in 1991.

DAN DAVE

WHO'S THE WORLD'S GREATEST ATHLETE?

DAN'S SHOES

DAVE'S SHOES

Dan and I hangin' tough with Sinbad during the filming of a Reebok commercial in early 1992.

Left page

Both Dan and I had a lot of fun with Reebok's "Who's the World's Greatest Athlete?" campaign.

Right page

Background: I couldn't believe all the people and cameras it took to make a commercial.

A. Dan and I rehearse our lines in a practice run before filming.

B. A crew member gives me the spray treatment to make it look like I've been sweating.

A

B

A

ALERION FIELD
Coca-Cola CLASSIC diet Coke Sprite
ane
THE ROAD TO BARCELONA
TAD GORMLEY STADIUM
U.S. Olympic Track & Field Trials
NI

B

Waiting between events at the 1992 Olympic Trials in New Orleans.

Left page

A. The Trials were the final step before the 1992 Olympics in Barcelona.

B. Sheri, her mom, and Coach Franson's wife, along with Reebok people, show their support.

Background: Ever-loyal fan Sheri waits patiently for me to get done with everyone else.

Right page

Background: The hurdles started off my best second-day score ever in competition.

A. I had a good pole vault—but Dan didn't. I would be going to Barcelona alone.

A

A

B

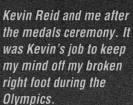

Kevin Reid and me after the medals ceremony. It was Kevin's job to keep my mind off my broken right foot during the Olympics.

Left page

Background: Taking the bronze medal at the Olympics was not what I'd set out to do. But I'd given my best.

A. I knew I hadn't fouled my third try at the shot put, but convincing the officials wasn't easy.

B. After it's all over Sheri and I take time for a group photo with our parents and her brother Michael in the Reebok hospitality room.

Right page

A. Katie Couric of the *Today* show wears my medal and shows off her biceps.

Background: Since the Olympics I've had the chance to speak to lots of kids. I tell them to go for their goals with all their heart, and to hang on when the going gets tough.

A

The Decathlon: Ten Grueling Events

1. 100-meter dash
2. Long jump
3. Shot put
4. High jump
5. 400 meters
6. 110-meter hurdles
7. Discus
8. Pole vault
9. Javelin
10. 1500 meters

Sharing a quiet moment with Alexandra before the final events of the Jeep Superstars competition.

Track and Field in 1992.) Like the Trials, you must have attained, at that time, a score of 7700 to qualify, so most of the best decathletes in the country were there. The experience I'd gained at the Trials in '84 and the previous month at the NAIA nationals helped me, and I turned in a better performance this time, placing fourth with a score of 7911. I struggled again with the pole vault, but at least managed to clear one height—13'1½"—avoiding the loss of hundreds of points. The score gave me my first national ranking: fifth in the United States.

I had one more unfortunate experience with the pole vault at the Sports Festival meet in Baton Rouge, Louisiana—later known as the Olympic Festival. My confidence in the event was at an all-time low, and I no-heighted once again. This time I placed fifth out of six decathletes. Afterwards, I resolved not to let this disaster happen again. Coach and I worked very hard on my vaulting skills, and I would later get some extra help from Coach Bakley.

My national ranking qualified me for a very special honor that summer, however: a week-long decathlon camp at the Olympic Training Center in Colorado Springs. When I heard I was going, I ran to the phone to call my parents. Only eighteen months earlier I had told them that someday I'd go to the Olympic Training Center, and now it was actually going to happen. They were as excited as I was.

The program, spearheaded by former decathletes Fred Samara and Harry Marra, was intended to improve the U.S.'s world standing in the decathlon by bringing together our top decathletes for a week of specialized training. I was amazed at how highly organized and technical the program was. We worked with scientists, doctors, psychologists, and other specialists on every imaginable aspect of the decathlon. I learned all kinds of things about the way my muscles and bones—not to mention my mind—worked in the midst of competition. I also had a lot of fun getting to know the other athletes and enjoying the camaraderie. But most of all, I felt the exhilaration of just being at the Olympic Training Center, the place where

Olympians were made. One day I'd be one of those
Olympians, I told myself.

That week at the OTC gave me a major boost. I needed it
badly at that point, because I was now on my own and I felt
like I had nowhere to go. My eligibility for the Azusa track
team had expired, along with my scholarship money. Coach
Franson had assured me that I could still train with the team,
but I knew it wouldn't be the same. I had to come up with a
way to pay for the fall semester of school and continue my
training.

Through Fred Samara and the U.S. Olympic Committee, I
began receiving a $300-a-month stipend, which helped a little.
Plus, I kept up my security guard job. I was saving transportation costs by riding a motorcycle my dad had helped me buy
from Nate Oliverson. And it only cost me $100 a month to
share a house off campus with some APU friends. But I still
didn't have enough to cover tuition. What else could I do?

Then I had an idea. I wasn't ineligible to compete in *all*
sports—only track. Suppose I played a different sport? Maybe
I could qualify for scholarship money in football. Then I'd stay
in good shape and still be able to pay for school. So, when football practices began in August, I put on the pads again for the
first time in four years.

For the next two weeks, I did the "daily doubles"—two
grueling practices a day in the California heat. I asked to play
wide receiver as before, but the coaches said they needed a free
safety, so I tried to learn the various defensive maneuvers. I
think I could have learned to be good at free safety, but my
favorite position was still wide receiver. It was especially obvious when we did the defensive drills: I'd play the wide
receiver and the other guys would cover me. Well, they'd *try* to
cover me. Most of the time I could shake them off and easily
make the catch. After two weeks of daily doubles, we began to
scrimmage as a team, with our full offense playing our full
defense.

Now it just so happened that my fellow janitor and Azusa
track team member, Christian Okoye, had decided to give foot-

ball a try this year. He immediately established himself as an awesome running back, bulldozing his way through the defensive line, shaking tackles left and right. While I was playing free safety during one of our scrimmages, I saw Christian get loose up the middle. He had blown by all the defenders, and I realized I was the last guy between him and the goal line. Would I be a pansy and let him go by? Make a half-hearted stab at a tackle? No way. I'd take him head on—I'd show him I wasn't afraid to hit and hit hard.

Boom.

The next thing I knew, I was lying flat on my back. Christian had steamrolled right over me. We had collided so hard that I didn't even have time to get hurt; I merely sat there stunned for a moment. Luckily, I'd gotten tangled up in his feet as he passed over and managed to bring him down, but it wasn't pretty.

That was on a Friday. Over the weekend I did some serious thinking. Even though the jolt from Christian hadn't injured me, I couldn't get it out of my mind. It made me realize that things can happen on the gridiron that wouldn't happen on the track, especially to someone like me who played so fiercely and fearlessly. In track and field, a fearless attitude translated into better results, but in football, it could easily get me hurt. I pictured myself breaking my arm or popping my knee, bringing my athletic career to a screeching halt. Since I knew the decathlon was my calling, I wondered about the wisdom of risking injury.

On Monday morning I told the coach I was through with football.

He tried to talk me out of it. In fact, he even offered to let me play wide receiver if I'd stay with the team. But I knew I was doing the right thing—I needed to save my body for track. Christian Okoye had definitely knocked some sense into me. (Several years later I asked him about that collision, and he didn't even remember it; it was just another play for him. I guess that shows what *his* calling was.) When I thought about it, my decision wasn't really a choice between the decathlon and football anyway, but between the decathlon and money. I'd gone out for football primarily because I wanted scholarship money to stay in school, not because I wanted to change sports.

After Christian's course correction, however, I still needed to work, train, and keep up in my fall classes. It was a difficult semester; nothing seemed to go right. Coach Franson treated me as if I was still on the team, and I practiced with them each day, but I always felt on the outside. There were plenty of people around to provide support—future Olympian Innocent Egbunike, Mike Barnett, and other track alums who still trained with the team—but I couldn't muster a positive attitude. Emotionally, I was finding it hard to be on my own.

On top of it, I did terribly in my classes. Eligibility was no longer an issue, so I wasn't feeling the same pressure to keep my grades up. When I went to my guard job at night, I'd bring my books along and try to study while I sat on my motorcycle. All I had to do was show up at an assigned location—a building or a construction site—and simply keep an eye on the place through the night. The study plan didn't work very well; I was too tired most of the time. I even went home early some nights and simply fell into bed. By Christmas my grades were so poor that I reluctantly withdrew from all my classes. In one course, I missed the deadline for withdrawal and had to take an F, which bothered me a lot. It was the first F I'd gotten in college.

I did have some good times, however. I enjoyed living with my Azusa friends Ron Buck, Ron Unger, Nate Oliverson, and several others on the second floor of a house near campus. And I was still going out with Sheri, who was now a sophomore. She had been a great support during my academic and financial struggles. Neither of us had money for fancy dates, so we took a lot of walks. She'd run track in high school herself, so occasionally she'd go running with me at night. Sheri insists to this day that once we were engaged I wouldn't run with her because she was too slow, but I sure appreciated her company that fall.

While home in Corvallis during Christmas vacation, I spent some time working on the pole vault with Coach Bakley at Linn-Benton. I never wanted to repeat the no-heighting experience I'd had twice the past year. When I returned to Azusa, I decided not to enroll for spring semester classes. I knew I would complete my psychology major eventually, but I didn't want bad grades, and I needed to get in great shape for the new track season. During the next three months, I trained with the team. Coach Franson continued as my coach, always affirming me and urging me not to give up. My workouts seemed to go well; I saw improvement in the various events, but I had to struggle to keep my focus.Whenever we went to meets, it still felt weird. The rules allowed me to compete, but only as an individual. I'd see my friends with Azusa Pacific on their chests, and I'd feel cut off from everyone.

I had picked up a sponsor, though. After the Olympic Trials in '84, Puma, a sneaker company, had started sending me shoes a couple of times a year. So I'd worn Pumas during my last season at APU. Now that I was on my own, I continued using their shoes and wore a Puma Track Club jersey. But even though the shoes gave me plenty of foot support, they gave me absolutely no emotional support, the thing I really needed. Fears and worries flowed through my head about where my life was going, and whether I'd really be able to make it as a decathlete.

My first decathlon of 1986 was the annual Fresno State Decathlon. The insecurity and self-doubt I was feeling clearly affected my performance: I posted only 7791. And a few weeks after that came the California Invitational sponsored by Azusa— the same meet in which I'd scored 8043 two years before. I took first place, but only managed a measly score of 7635.

What a major disappointment. *Man,* I wondered, *maybe the Lord's telling me my time's up for the decathlon. Maybe I just need to quit training, get a job, and finish school. I guess I'm supposed to serve God in a regular career instead of the decathlon.*

But something stopped me from believing those words— a feeling from within that I think came from the Lord. *Don't give up yet, Dave,* was the message. *It's going to be OK. Don't be afraid of being alone, of not being on the track team, of not being in school. Give it another try—not a half effort, but your very best effort. Then, if you have to walk away from the decathlon at least you'll know you gave it your best shot.*

I decided to trust God and give myself one more chance. The U.S. Championships were coming up in June in Eugene, Oregon. For the next two months, I would train harder than I'd ever trained in my life, and then go for broke in that meet. If I didn't do well, I'd accept it as an indication from God that it was time to quit the decathlon and move on with my life.

■ ■ ■

There were several other matters I also needed to consider at this point. Sheri, for one. Our two-year dating relationship had grown into love, and I knew I wanted to marry her, but I didn't feel right about asking her until my future and my financial condition were more stable.

I also had to scramble for a new place to live, since several of the guys were moving out of the house and I couldn't afford higher rent. At that time Azusa Pacific had just sold the hillside campus, where the track was located, and was in the process of building a new track down on the main campus. Besides the gym and the old dirt track, the upper campus also had a small dormitory, Ike Hall, which now stood empty. I had heard that the buyer, the Church of the Open Door, would not begin renovations for some time, so I wondered if they'd allow me to live up there in exchange for watching the property. With much help from Coach Franson and others in the Azusa administration, I was able to work it out. From the end of April through September, I stayed there rent-free. It couldn't have come at a better time.

Although I'd never lived on the hillside campus, I'd done so many workouts on that track that I felt at home up there. Now I had the whole place to myself, other than a few church people who came around during the day. Ike Hall's tiny rooms looked like jail cells, but they were certainly livable, especially for the price I was paying. I was even allowed to use the swimming pool. Nate Oliverson and Ron Buck soon moved in with me, and we had ourselves one cool hangout. Since all three of us had motorcycles, we decided to change the name of the dorm from Ike Hall to Bike Hall. We even made the change "official" by taking adhesive tape and adding a large "B" to the sign in front of the building.

Bike Hall was a fun place, but I especially liked being right next to the track and the hills where I trained all the time. Whenever I wanted I could step out the door and take off running. Sheri was working as a summer intern in a hospital in San Diego, so I used our time apart to the maximum. I worked my butt off those two months, training harder than I'd ever done before. First thing every morning, high above the L.A. rat race, I'd sprint up and down the fire road, again, again, again, feeling better about my conditioning and better about myself. And Coach still kept all the equipment up there for me to use. It was a time to be alone with myself and with God. I grew much more focused and confident, and much less afraid. Mostly, I think I grew up. My future wasn't any clearer to me, but my instincts told me that if I gave my very best at the U.S. Championships, afterwards—win or lose—I'd know what to do next.

The TAC National Championships were held in Eugene on June 18–19. Since my parents lived only an hour away, they joined the small group of spectators, which numbered a few hundred at most. Sheri's parents also came to watch me compete for the first time. I wanted to impress them, because I figured they were probably wondering about this guy their daughter was dating who had dropped out of school and didn't have a steady job. I wanted to show them I was serious about the decathlon and serious about Sheri. My sister Lois got married around the date of the meet, so a pack of relatives also showed up at the meet. Roger and Barb had moved to Corvallis, and Roger made up a batch of "Go Dave" t-shirts with my picture on it. Quite a cheering section.

After all my training on the hill, I felt completely ready for this meet. I wasn't going to let anything distract me. I didn't care that several of the country's top-ranked decathletes had passed on this meet to rest up for the Goodwill Games. Neither did I let the predictably unpredictable Oregon weather throw me. Outdoors it was mostly cloudy, and rained on and off; there was even an occasional rattling of hail. Inside of me, however, the sun was blazing.

I felt strong in almost every event, finishing the first day in the lead with a better-than-average score of 4133. I PR'd in the long jump by nine inches, and two events later PR'd in the high jump. And then came a moment I'll never forget. It occurred during the high jump, when the bar was raised to 6'9½"—a height I'd never cleared. As I stood there preparing to make my approach, the voice of announcer Frank Zarnowski came over the PA: "If Dave Johnson makes this jump, he will literally leap into the lead." His comment got me so fired up that I cleared it on my first attempt.

Once I leaped into the lead, I never lost it. On the second day, another PR in the discus (151'5") gave me additional insurance, and I won the meet with a total score of 8203, my highest ever.

I could hardly contain my excitement. Barely two months ago I'd almost given up the decathlon for good. Now, suddenly, I was the U.S. champion.

That victory was one of the biggest turning points in my career—in my life. God had answered all my doubts, all my questions, all my fears, with a clear message: Yes, I'm with you and I'm taking care of you. Yes, the decathlon is part of your future. Yes, you can be confident in pursuing it as long as you put me first.

I felt so grateful. During this uncertain year, the Lord had brought me to a new level not only in my sport, but in my self-understanding. He continued to be with me even after I had stepped out from under the protection of the track team and the sheltering of Azusa Pacific University. For three years now they had been like a second family to me—the friends, the teachers, Coach Franson, athletic director Cliff Hamlow, football coach Jim Milhon, soccer coach Don Lawrence, dean of students John Wallace, and many others. They'd done practically everything with me that a family could do—nurtured my faith, taught me, disciplined me, supported me, laid the groundwork for my future, put up with my many rough edges, even provided for me financially. I could never have gotten as far as I had in the decathlon without them—no question about it. Every victory I'd won belonged as much to them as it did to me.

But just as I had to leave my mom and dad in order to grow up and find my life purpose, I also had to "leave" my Azusa family to find my true source of motivation. They couldn't give it to me; their friendship and support, as important as it was, would not in itself make me a great decathlete. The real motivation, the rock-bottom reason for going after the decathlon had to come from within myself. It had to arise out of my own desire to serve God.

With this realization came a whole new sense of freedom and awareness of my potential. With Christ as my driving purpose, I began to see my place in the world. I saw value in who I could become. If I put my faith in him and gave one hundred percent of myself—in sports and in life—there would be no limit to what I could accomplish for him.

Up to this point I had just wanted to be good at the decathlon. But now I no longer wanted simply to be good—I wanted to be the best. After all, would Christ want me to strive for anything less? If *he* were a decathlete, there'd be no scoring tables high enough to accommodate him. And since my calling was to be as much like Christ as I could, I shouldn't place any limits on what I could score, either.

■ ■ ■

The confidence I'd gained through my hill training and the victory in Eugene also spurred me to take the next step in my relationship with Sheri. I was ready to ask for her hand in marriage. Even though I didn't know *exactly* how my life would go, I felt secure enough in the direction God was pointing. As national decathlon champion, I figured I'd be able to earn enough money from sponsors to support my wife and me. Before the championship meet, I'd heard a song on the radio.

One of the phrases in it went, "I want to be your knight in shining armor." That's what I wanted to be for Sheri—an inspiration, someone she could look up to, someone who would take care of her. By winning that meet, I felt like I was showing her I could be that kind of person. So I watched for an opportunity to pop the question. One of my track buddies and I started to work on a plan where I would take Sheri to the beach, and he'd come up from the ocean with some lobsters and cook a romantic dinner for us right there. Then afterwards I'd ask her to marry me.

Finding the time to carry out our plan wasn't easy, however, because things started to move quickly after Eugene. The win established me as a leading U.S. decathlete, and qualified me to compete in other national and even international meets. First came the Olympic Festival in Houston on August 2 and 3. After a "break" of several days, I would spend another week at the Olympic Training Center, and then in September I'd fly to Talence, France, for my first international competition.

During July I took a few days off from training to visit Sheri in San Diego, where she'd been staying with her Grandma and Grandpa Burgess. So much had happened to me in the many weeks since I'd seen her that I hardly knew where to start catching up. We had talked on the phone, of course, but I'd really missed being with her. Now I was able to tell her in person about all the great opportunities that were opening up for me. I was going to travel, and now that I was ranked second in the U.S. I would probably earn more money. I had a clearer sense of the direction God wanted me to go with my life. Many of the specifics remained unknown, but I felt confident that I was moving forward with God's blessing. Over the past year, the Polaroid photo of my life hadn't seemed to be developing very quickly, but now the image was becoming clearer.

One of the evenings I was there Sheri made a great spaghetti dinner, and the two of us had just finished eating. She looked so beautiful that night, and the prospects of married life with her looked so good to me, that I suddenly heard myself asking her right then and there to marry me.

She was happy, but wanted to be sure I wasn't joking, so she told me to write it down on paper. So I grabbed a pen and wrote, "Sheri, I really do want to marry you. You are the one for me. Please take my hand in marriage forever."

Her answer was yes. But I'd have to call her father first to make it official. I was very nervous, but her dad was great and gave his immediate support.

My confidence now soared—all the way to Houston and the Olympic Festival—formerly the Sports Festival. It's called the Olympic Festival because it's set up to give athletes the experience of being in a big meet. This was the same meet I'd no-heighted in the year before. In the sweltering heat exceeding 100 degrees, I took first place with a score of 8134. Victory was sweet, but did not come without a little scare: I only managed 15'1" in the pole vault, which cost me eighty or ninety points, and even after tossing a PR of 218' with the new javelin, I was only three points ahead of second-place Gary Kinder. But I ran a solid 1500 meters and ended up winning by 125 points.

Within days of the Festival I found myself in Colorado Springs at the Olympic Training Center for the second time. I wanted to work some more on my speed, so I did all sorts of drills and underwent tests on a treadmill for lung capacity and lactic acid buildup. Again, it was a great experience.

The last few weeks of the summer seemed to fly by, and before I knew it I was flying again, this time to Talence, France, as one of six American decathletes selected to compete in the annual international meet. It was the first time I'd ever traveled outside of North America, and I was especially psyched—not only because of the new opportunity, but also because Coach Franson was coming along. He'd been appointed one of the U.S. coaches for the team. I would shortly discover just how crucial his presence was.

I charged into the meet with a good time in the 100 meters. However, in only the second event, the long jump, I ran into a problem. I'd been jumping tremendously far in practice—farther than I'd ever jumped in my life. But in my excitement, I ran a little too aggressively and fouled my first two jumps. If even the slightest portion of your shoe extends past the board, you've fouled. And if you foul three times, you get zero points for that event.

For my last attempt I tried to settle down and back my step up, but I was running so hard that I felt like I was going to foul again. As soon as my foot pounded the board and sent me into the air, I thought for sure I'd gone over the line. *Oh man, I fouled*, I thought. Apparently the crowd thought so too, because I heard them groan, "Ohhhhhh." It's amazing how much you can think about during one split second in the air. Putting two and two together—my own gut feeling and the noise of the crowd—I was sure I'd fouled, and I stepped down on one foot and ran out of the jump. I had just no-marked in my second event and blown the entire meet.

But then I heard Coach Franson shouting at me. "Dave, what are you *doing*?" he yelled in exasperation. "That was a legal jump!"

It was? Sure enough, the officials had made no foul call. They simply measured from the spot where my one foot had landed. The distance, 20'3", was nearly four feet short of my best at that time. Had I stretched out the jump, I would have probably gotten closer to 25 feet. While I still got 600-some points for the event instead of zero, I *could* have easily gotten 900 if I hadn't dropped my foot.

Despairing over my mistake, I immediately wanted to quit the meet. *Why go through the pain of this decathlon when I know I'm not gonna win*, I thought. *I'm not gonna come even close to winning because I lost so many points.*

Coach Franson, ever the encourager, sat me down. "Dave, don't give up yet, it's way too early," he said. "You've gotta trust me on this one. You know in the decathlon anything can happen—somebody else could drop out or blow an event. Stick with it, and you might still be OK. Who knows? You might even win."

I didn't really want to, but I thought, *OK, I'll do what he says.* After each event I wanted to quit again; I felt like I was wasting my time. If I didn't have a chance to win, why bother?

Nevertheless, Coach kept urging me to continue. I garnered respectable scores for the rest of the day's events, but I wasn't really paying attention.

On the second day, I ran a fast hurdles, one of my better times. *Too bad it didn't matter*, I thought. Then, after throwing a strong discus, it suddenly occurred to me: *Wait a minute—I'm catching up with these guys!* Some of the leaders were faltering, just as Coach had said, and I was getting stronger. A PR in the pole vault brought me up to eighth or ninth in the standings. And a great throw in the javelin landed me in fourth. Finally, I ran a solid 1500 meters and ended up in third place with a score of 7841. In my first international meet, I'd won a bronze medal. And the winner, Christian Plaziat of France, had scored only 100 points or so more than me. If I had stayed focused and completed that last long jump, I could very well have won the whole meet.

Coach had been right. Without his encouragement, I'm sure I would have quit. He had taken a potential disaster and made it not only into a winning performance, but also a positive learning experience.

■   ■   ■

Back in Azusa after a whirlwind summer, I resumed my training, this time with the APU team on their beautiful new track. Innocent Egbunike and I often ran together. Another training friend was Kevin Reid, an Azusa student who ran hurdles; he would later become a special friend and play a key role in my decathlon career. By this time I'd moved from Bike Hall with Nate down to an apartment near campus. Sheri, now a junior, stopped over often and we began making wedding plans. It was great to spend time with her again after an entire summer apart. We settled on a date of June 12, 1987, which seemed to work best for the families. I was a little nervous that only eleven days later I'd be defending my U.S. decathlon title at the TAC National Championships, but I figured everything would work out. The meet would be sort of a honeymoon for us.

To support myself, I continued the part-time security job and mowed lawns for a gardening service. I'd been able to scrape by on my own, but now that I would soon be supporting Sheri as well, I wanted to provide a reasonable income and still be able to train. Fred Samara and the U.S. Olympic Committee had been sending me $300 a month for the past year, and doubled the amount to $600 when I won in Eugene. That was a big help, but still not enough for a married couple to live on in Southern California.

I began writing letters to all kinds of companies that I thought would be interested in sponsoring me. Shortly after winning the U.S. championship I'd contacted Puma, who'd been sending me shoes for the past two years. They'd treated my friend Innocent Egbunike well financially. In fact, he was the one who had first asked them to send me shoes. Surely they'd be willing to kick in a few hundred dollars a month to help me train for the Olympics, especially now that I had a national title.

I could hardly believe my eyes when I read their curt letter of reply: Not only would they be unable to send any money, but they had also decided to stop sending me shoes. They weren't interested in sponsoring decathletes.

That letter provided me with a rude introduction to the world of athletic sponsorships. I was hurt, but I just knew that there were companies out there who'd want me. I scanned the ads in magazines, looking for products I thought I could represent. I wrote dozens of letters in which I explained who I was, listed some of my decathlon accomplishments—with the national championship at the top—and then asked for their help. "I'm going to go to the 1988 Olympic Games, and I'm going to win," I wrote. Then I'd explain how I'd promote their product, how it would benefit their company, and so on.

The first company to respond was Nike, who had also sponsored another decathlete, Tim Bright. After Tim put in a good word for me, they agreed to send shoes and sports clothing regularly—much more than Puma. And while they didn't send any money, they offered to pay me bonuses of $1,000 and up for winning various national and international titles or for being ranked in the top five in the U.S. Well, it wouldn't pay the rent, but it was a start.

I also contacted the New York Athletic Club (NYAC) at the suggestion of John Sayre, another decathlete I'd competed with. The people there were very kind and professional, especially Tommy Quinn, my main contact. He explained that while they didn't provide monthly support for athletes, they'd be glad to help with occasional travel expenses if I'd wear their jersey. He also gave me a complimentary membership to their classy Manhattan facility and said I could stay there free whenever I came to New York.

Another positive sign, but I needed more, so I kept up my fundraising campaign.

In late fall of 1986 I was sitting on a plane to Gainesville, Florida, for an indoor pentathlon meet. Flipping through the airline magazine, I noticed an ad for Blublocker sunglasses. Hmm—sunglasses. I wore sunglasses all the time. Maybe they'd be interested in sponsoring me. When I returned home, I dialed the 800 number in the ad, got a name and address, and sent a letter to their home office in Chicago.

A few weeks later I received several pairs of Blublockers in the mail with a friendly note saying, "Wear these sunglasses when you're out on the track—they'll help you a lot." So I did, and you know what? They really were good sunglasses. I wrote back to thank them and enclosed pictures of me wearing Blublockers while I pole vaulted.

Then one day, after several more cordial contacts, the phone rang. It was Joseph Sugarman, president of Blublocker sunglasses. He wanted to fly to California to meet me and talk about the possibility of doing a commercial. *Whoa*, I thought, *a commercial? This is too cool.* Sure enough, they decided to include me in a half-hour "infomercial" in which I pole vaulted, ran hurdles, and talked about Blublocker sunglasses. In exchange, they'd send me $100 a month straight through the '88 Olympic Games—and of course, all the Blublockers I needed.

I thought it was a phenomenal deal. After all, I wasn't anything close to being a public figure. I'd won two national meets, but I hadn't ever been to the Olympics, and there was no guarantee I'd make the '88 team. So I viewed the Blublockers sponsorship as one of God's ways of assuring me my life was on the right track. It made me believe he wanted me to be the best. It motivated me to work harder. The company filmed the infomercial in March, right at Azusa.

To keep myself in top form for the U.S. championships, I competed in Azusa's California Invitational Decathlon in early April. My training had been going so well that I cruised right through the meet and easily won with a score of 8045. Now I could be even more confident for the June TAC nationals in San Jose.

Little did I know that the California Invitational meet would be my last major competition for more than a year.

■　■　■

It's difficult to get injured in track and field.

Difficult, but not impossible.

It happened very innocuously during a practice in early May. I'd been working on the shotput with Coach Franson and the team. I had just taken a throw, and I stepped out of the ring as usual. Unfortunately, I didn't notice that another shot had rolled up alongside the ring, and I stepped on it, twisting my right ankle. It hurt a little, but no big deal, I thought. I decided to give it a rest for the day.

The next day I resumed training. My ankle was slightly swollen and a little sore, but I didn't want to back off from my regimen, so I went ahead and ran my workouts. For the next week and a half, the soreness lingered, never quite going away. Then the pain began to increase, a little each day, then a little more, until it really started bothering me.

Finally, I went for an x-ray. The doctors couldn't find any visible problem with the bones, however, so they concluded that I had a bone spur—a tiny splinter of bone that can aggravate nerve endings and cause a great deal of pain. Hang in there, they told me, and it would probably go away on its own. So I taped up my ankle each day and tried to continue training, but the pain refused to go away. In fact, it grew worse. By the first week of June, I was limping so badly that I had to stop working out altogether.

Here I was, one week away from getting married and three weeks away from the U.S. championships. I was looking forward to the wedding and the beginning of married life with Sheri, but I also felt preoccupied with my foot.

We had a fun and beautiful wedding at Sweet Home Mennonite Church in Sweet Home, Oregon. My brother, Gary, served as Best Man, and Coach Franson, my brother-in-law Roger, Ron Buck, and Nate were groomsmen. Sheri's sister, Sheli, was Maid of Honor (she would later marry Nate), and her friend Bobby Baine was one of the bridesmaids.

Sheri looked absolutely stunning coming down the aisle. But as I stood next to her facing the minister, I couldn't help but feel the nagging pain in my ankle. I tried to put it out of my mind and enjoy the occasion. Lots of our friends from APU came, which only added to the merriment. I gave Blublocker sunglasses to the entire wedding party, and we wore them for some of the pictures. Coach Bakley was there too, and I introduced him to Coach Franson for the first time.

After the wedding reception we jumped into Sheri's "new" car, an early-'70s Plymouth Satellite Sebring, metallic blue. She'd bought it from her grandfather, and called it "The Shark" because of its pointed shape in front. Our friends had completely decorated it with all the proper gaudy words and attachments, and they'd loaded up all my equipment, our luggage, and a heap of wedding gifts. As a joke, they strapped my vaulting poles right on to the driver's side so I had to contort myself to get into the car. We almost looked like the Beverly Hillbillies as we pulled away.

Our plan was to spend Saturday and Sunday nights in a cozy bed and breakfast about two hours away. Then on Monday we'd return to Corvallis for a few days before trekking down to the big meet in San Jose.

The wedding night was a dream.

The second night was a disaster. We'd gone out for dinner, and either I got food poisoning or a violent case of the flu, because I was socked with twenty-four straight hours of vomiting and diarrhea, followed by another twenty-four hours recovering in bed. I had completely dehydrated myself and felt quite weak for the next three or four days. Sheri took care of me on the honeymoon and in Corvallis until I felt strong enough to leave. It was great to have a nurse for a bride, but I hadn't thought I'd need her services so quickly. Sheri's dad said, "So Dave, is my daughter too much for you?"

No, she wasn't, but the pain in my ankle turned out to be. Down in San Jose at the TAC nationals, I limped through the first day with a very subpar score. On the second day, the sore ankle and the lingering weakness from being sick took their toll. I stumbled during the hurdles and placed dead last, then followed up with a mediocre discus throw. I was hurting too much to go any further. For the first time in my career I had to drop out of a meet.

Afterwards I was disappointed, but not depressed. I could point to a specific reason for my problem—the bone spur. Before long it would go away and I'd be fine. Since I didn't complete the nationals, there would be no Olympic Festival or no international competition for me this season. But Coach Franson worked it out for me to compete as a "guest" at the USA v. Canada meet in Saskatoon, Saskatchewan. The doctors suggested that I take it easy on my foot, try the August decathlon in Canada, and see how it felt. If it still hurt after that, they'd go in and surgically remove the bone spur.

Meanwhile, Sheri and I settled into married life. We had found a duplex in Covina that was convenient to school and Sheri's summer job at a local hospital. We got along great and both really enjoyed being married. I've heard some people say that the first year of marriage is the worst, but for us it was spectacular.

Financially, we managed to squeak by. Soon after we were married, Joseph Sugarman had called us and said he was going to add another "0" onto the $100 a month we were getting from them. The extra money helped, but between the Blublockers sponsorship and the USOC subsidy, I was still only pulling in an annual "salary" of less than $15,000—adequate for Montana, perhaps, but quite low for metropolitan Los Angeles's high cost of living. On top of it, we needed to pay for Sheri's senior year at Azusa Pacific. But ever since I'd asked her to marry me, I had a feeling that God would allow me to be the best in the decathlon some day, and that my achievements would eventually support us financially.

Soon after our wedding I received confirmation of that feeling when I learned that I would be getting work through the Olympic Job Opportunity Program. It gave me a half-time job with a corporate Olympic sponsor for which I'd receive a full-time salary ($1,800 a month) and complete medical benefits. That way I'd still be able to train each day. Sheri and I were amazed at how the Lord was providing for us. It was as if he was saying, "Okay Dave, I want you to be free from having to worry too much about finances so you can train and be focused."

I think he was also letting us know he had a sense of humor. When I heard where I'd be working, I couldn't help but laugh: at the Van Nuys offices of Anheuser-Busch—as in Budweiser, the company I'd "patronized" so frequently in Missoula. My duties would involve simple office tasks such as filing and answering phones, and occasional public relations activities.

In August I traveled with Coach Franson to Saskatoon for the USA/Canada meet, a low-key competition with nothing major at stake. I didn't have to go, but I felt like I needed to in order to keep up my confidence and attract potential sponsors. If I did well, it would also help my national ranking.

I had thought my foot would be better by now, but it killed me for the entire meet. At several points along the way I considered dropping out again. Somehow, though, I just gutted it out and endured the pain. With everything the Lord had been doing for me, I really wanted to give him everything I had in this competition. When it was all over, I'd won the whole meet with a score of 7824, which gave me a ranking of eighth in the U.S.

It felt good to win, but I knew something was still wrong with my foot. So I decided to go ahead with the surgery to remove the bone spur. The operation took place in September, and the doctors felt that the procedure had been a success. Sheri took time out of her studies to help me through my recovery, which lasted about a month. We were such good friends, and I felt like we were now a team, working together to serve God. In spite of being incapacitated for a time, I felt optimistic that my foot would heal soon and everything would be fine.

I slowly resumed my training in November and December, beginning with low-impact exercise such as cycling. Then I started back in with my normal workouts, assuming I'd be able to pound on my foot again. But any time I ran hard or tried to do hills, the ankle still hurt a lot, as if something was still wrong with it. Maybe it was scar tissue, or simply a longer-than-usual time to heal, the doctors theorized. The soreness would go away eventually. So I just kept up the training and hoped it would improve.

For the most part, 1987 was a lost season. I now had barely six months to finish healing and get in shape for the 1988 Olympic Trials. Not a great situation to be in, but for some reason I felt hopeful. God had clearly been with me in so many ways, confirming my life direction again and again. Even though I didn't understand why he allowed me to get injured, I sensed that he was using this "down time" to build my character. Yes, he cared about my health and my performance as an athlete, but he cared even more about the person I was becoming on the inside. Maybe he was telling me that in order to reach my goal of being the best, I'd need to work as hard on my inner person as I did on the outer athlete.

Discus

PR: 163'8"

Remember the ancient Greek statue of the discus thrower? The event looks strikingly similar today, except that they make us wear clothes.

Not to be confused with a Frisbee, the discus is about as thick as two Frisbees glued rim to rim, and it weighs a lot more—almost 5 pounds. The whirling of the thrower and the spinning of the disc make it a beautiful event to watch and perform. You really need to make your body work in order to send the discus into flight.

The event does not physically tax you or cause pain like many of the others, but it does involve a certain amount of technique. Part of the challenge stems from the condition your body's in at this point in the competition. Your legs are still trying to recover from the first day and from just pounding over the hurdles. They're a little wobbly, and they remind you of the sleep you didn't get last night. As the discus begins, you find yourself relaxing a little—the last thing you should feel if you want to do well. But if you can get yourself excited, the discus is a lot more fun and the results a lot better, too.

The other challenge is staying within a two-and-a-half-meter circle (slightly over eight feet), which, like the shot put circle, can be restrictive. Fouls are common. It's hard to spin, keep your feet inside the line, and still get a good throw—so hard for some decathletes that they'll settle for a short, "safe" throw and lose a lot of points.

I'm especially intrigued by all the circular images and movements in the discus event. You stand in a circle, rotate your body in a circle, throw a circular disc, and put a circular spin on it. The spinning of your body and of the disc gives you more energy, more distance.

The discus also helps me overcome lethargy. Just as we have to turn over the car engine a few times to start it, or wind an old-fashioned watch for it to run, we may also need to get ourselves "wound up" in order to generate as much energy as possible for certain tasks. There are times in life when all of us grow tired. We may feel weak on the outside, even though deep down we know we could do much better. The discus reminds to do more than "just get by." It tells me I need to draw my inner strength from God and to "think I can." What an exciting and productive experience that can be!

■ ■ ■

■ chapter eight ■

NO BIZ LIKE SHOE BIZ

AFTER MY ANKLE SURGERY in September of 1987, I did not compete in any decathlons until the U.S. Olympic Trials in Indianapolis, Indiana the following July. As it turned out, I wouldn't even have qualified for the Trials if I hadn't picked up the 7824 score in Saskatoon the previous summer.

I trained the best I could, but with minimal success. With the help of physical therapist John Wallace, I taped up my foot and tried to run, but I still experienced too much pain to get into the kind of shape I needed to be in. As the spring months of 1988 passed, I began to worry that I wouldn't be able to compete in the Trials at all.

What neither I nor the doctors knew during that time was that the problem with my ankle had not been a bone spur. I'd actually broken a bone in my ankle—the navicular bone, which formed the instep of my right foot. Either I'd fractured it the moment I stepped on that shot, or possibly I'd knocked it out of adjustment and then fractured it afterwards when I ran on it. This type of injury is known as a stress fracture, and it often doesn't show up on standard x-rays.

I know that now. I didn't know it then. Neither did I know how dramatically the injury would alter the course of my career.

About a month before the Trials, the pain suddenly stopped. Well, almost. I tried running, slowly at first, then

harder, then at full speed, and to my amazement, the foot felt
OK. I couldn't understand it, but I sure was thankful to be free
of pain for a change. Looking back, it may simply have taken
that long for the stress fracture to heal up enough to where I
could run on it. But maybe the Lord wanted me to learn a lesson in trust when I went to the Trials. Of course I knew that just
as faith without works is dead, in the decathlon faith without
workouts is dead, so I spent that last month training as hard as
I could. Even then, I wasn't in great shape for Indianapolis. I
would indeed have to exercise a lot of faith there in addition to
exercising my body.

The day finally arrived—July 20, 1988. An excellent cheering squad of family had flown in for the occasion: Sheri, her
mom, my parents, my brother-in-law Roger, and my brother,
Gary. Sheri and her mom shared a room with Coach Franson's
wife, Nancy, and I stayed with Coach. When I got up that
morning, I looked out my hotel window and saw rain—not a
drizzle, not a shower, but a downpour. It's always a bummer
to do some of the events, especially the shot put and high
jump, in the rain, but I tried to keep my spirits up.

I was nervous. It's scary enough to be facing the meet of
your life—where you have to perform at your very best just to
make the team. Not to mention standing before the largest
crowd a decathlete will ever see outside of the Olympic Games
itself. But I also had the added factor of utterly miserable
weather conditions that could seriously affect the outcome of
the meet. It would be much easier to slip, foul, fall, or suffer
injury.

Torrential rains delayed the start of the 100 meters for an
hour. Then an hour and a half. Then two hours. While we waited, I was able to say hello to some of the other decathletes,
many of whom I'd already competed against: Tim Bright, Gary
Kinder, John Sayre, and others. Finally, the rain let up a little,
and we lined up for the first heat. (It should have been called
the first *bath*.) We'd hardly walked out on the track when it
began to pour again, but the officials decided that the show
must go on. As I stepped into the blocks, I prayed, *Lord, help me*

to give one hundred percent. Please allow me to make this Olympic team. I wanted to make the team, and I was going to give it my all, but I knew I had to leave the outcome in his hands.

If there's anything worse than running in the rain, it's running into the wind. This particular morning I had both. I turned in a decent, but not spectacular, time of 11.14. My ankle, which had been heavily taped, held up extremely well. Since the tape got soaked, however, it had to be removed after each event and replaced with dry tape.

One young athlete raised eyebrows by running 10.83, only a hundredth of a second out of first. His name was Dan O'Brien, someone I'd never heard of before. He did only one more event before dropping out with an injury.

The monsoon showed no signs of subsiding as we practically waded up to the long jump area. Huge puddles were forming everywhere, and each time I jumped there was a big splash. I was actually able to sit down in one of the deeper puddles to wash off the sand from the long jump pit. Again, I was pleasantly surprised by my performance—third best with a distance of 24'1½".

Next came the shot put. What a joke. The throwing circle had become a kiddie pool, and even after great vacuums were used to suck out the water, the athletes slipped and fouled through the event. Once we were able to get off a throw, the shot often sank completely into the mud, requiring officials to dig it out with a shovel. In spite of the absolutely terrible conditions, I still managed a good throw, placing fourth.

I continued with solid performances in the last two events—tying for second in the high jump (which had mercifully been moved indoors) and then running the second-best time in the 400 meters. By the end of the first waterlogged day, Gary, Tim, and I were in the top three positions.

And that's where we stayed, straight through the second day, which, thankfully, was sunny and warm. After setting a meet record with the new javelin—only to have it broken by Jim Connolly—and PRing in the 1500, I finished the Trials in third place with a score of 8245, less than fifty points out of first. I'd made the team.

What an incredible feeling. I'd made it to the big time. I was going to the Olympic Games to compete against the best in the world. I'll never forget the exhilaration of running my victory lap, American flag in hand, and waving to the packed stadium of 10,000. When I got around to where Sheri was sitting, she came down from the stands and gave me a big hug and a kiss. It felt so good to show her that one of the dreams I'd been telling her about had actually come true. That experience ranks as one of my life's most special moments. And Sheri admits that from that day on she became hooked on the decathlon.

My parents were so happy for me, so proud that I was accomplishing things in my life. Five or six years ago, they would have never dreamed they'd see me in anything but trouble. Now, here I was, about to take off for the Olympic Games.

Only a few weeks passed before Coach Franson and I packed up for Seoul. First we went with the entire U.S. Olympic team to a two-week training camp in Chiba, Japan. There we were able to adjust to the climate, which is very similar to Seoul's, the time zone, even Korean food which had been shipped in.

Most important, we trained in an extremely supportive and upbeat environment. I loved the entire experience—working out alongside the cream of America's athletes and their coaches. And we all wanted each other to win, so we freely shared whatever advice or technical tips we'd picked up. This probably helped me more than it helped the others: because all the track and field athletes who compete in open events were better than me, I could ask them or their coaches to watch me and then offer suggestions for improvement. I practiced the 1500 meters, for instance, by running with Pat Porter, who'd be doing the open 1500 meters at the Games. I hurdled with Roger Kingdom and pole vaulted with Kory Tarpenning, another one of Coach Bakley's Olympians.

My foot seemed pretty strong, though I continued taping it for good measure. Only a little soreness remained—more of an ache than the piercing pain I'd felt before. I was finally beginning to feel as if my body was in good shape, even if I didn't have the benefit of those spring training months. By the time the camp ended, I was very psyched for Seoul. I actually believed I could win. As I looked over the list of decathletes who'd be competing, I thought, *If I score 8500 to 8600, I could probably win this thing.* And I knew I was capable of doing it.

Of course, being *capable* of doing it and actually doing it are two different things. I would learn that the hard way in Seoul. There were other factors I hadn't yet learned to account for—the huge crowds, the TV cameras in your face, the burden of representing your country, the much larger field of decathletes, and the much longer waits between events. I felt some of that pressure during the Trials, but during the actual Games the pressure increased tenfold.

Some athletes can easily block out all these distractions, or else use them to their advantage. I was still learning how to stay focused. In fact, my entire time in Seoul was a great learning experience.

Not to mention fun and inspiring. Between and during some of the events, I enjoyed sitting down by the track with Tim Bright and taking in all the excitement. We'd become friends in the years since our first meeting at the 1984 Trials. He'd made the Olympic team that year and competed in Los Angeles, so this was his second Olympics. Tim had also attended Linn-Benton Community College and trained under Dave Bakley, giving us another area of common ground. Coach Bakley was even with him and Kory in Seoul, and cheered all three of us on.

Tim and I had a great moment during the pole vault competition. The vaulting takes forever, and while we waited for our turns, we watched the finish of the women's 200 meters. Florence Griffith-Joyner and her phosphorescent fingernails blew everyone away and broke the world record right before our eyes. Tim and I marveled at how incredibly fast she was, and how slow we were by comparison. We had the feeling of being witnesses to history. Remember the *Sports Illustrated* cover with Flo-Jo's husband and coach, Al Joyner, embracing her immediately after the race? We were barely fifteen feet away from that scene. Tim looked at me and said, "This is a pretty fun place to be, isn't it?"

The day after the decathlon had finished, Tim and I offered to sneak Coach Bakley into the athletes' village cafeteria for breakfast. We had told him that the food there was absolutely awful, and he didn't believe us, so we wanted him to experience it for himself. Since he didn't have the needed credentials, we used our own IDs to enter, then propped open a couple of doors and let him through. It was our own little Olympic prank.

He agreed with us about the food.

I met a number of other interesting people after the competition. One of the Olympic coaches, Irv "Moon" Mondschein, came up to me. He'd competed in the 1948 Olympics and had stayed involved with the decathlon ever since. Now in his sixties, he was a really nice guy who knew the decathlon inside out.

"Dave," he said, "I know Bright and those other guys beat you, but I can see something about you. You're gonna do very well." Something to that effect. His words meant a lot to me, because I knew that with the Lord's help, I had the potential to be the best. It felt good to have someone like him recognize that potential.

I also bumped into a legend among decathletes, Bob Mathias, who won back-to-back gold medals in the 1948 and 1952 Olympics. Sheri and I, along with both sets of our parents, were exploring the Itaewon, a huge shopping district in Seoul with incredibly low prices. Bob Mathias also happened to be there, and since he'd just watched me compete, he walked up and introduced himself. Even at fifty-seven, he looked strong and athletic. He had earned his first gold at the age of seventeen—in only the third decathlon of his life. And here he was, talking to me.

"Good job out there, Dave—congratulations," he said. "You've got a lot of potential. Keep training hard!" Then he went on his way, leaving me standing there with my mouth open. He would become a good friend in the years to come.

Sheri and I enjoyed several special times together in Seoul. She came as part of the Seagram's Send the Families Program, which provided free transportation, housing, and even spending money for one family member of each Olympic athlete. She stayed in the family Olympic village, sharing a room with the wife of another American athlete. Before the Olympics began, Mr. Lee, owner of the Blublocker factory in Seoul, graciously treated Sheri and me to one night in a luxurious hotel. It was definitely a highlight of the trip. We stayed in the huge Presidential Suite complete with robes and slippers, and ordered spaghetti (ah, normal food!) from room service. Then, a few days before the competition, I got a pass for her to hang out with me in the athletes' village, where we explored, took lots of pictures, and gagged on the terrible food. We both had a great time.

It was also fun to have both sets of our parents there, even though I didn't get to spend much time with them. Not only were they watching me in the Olympics for the first time, but they were also traveling out of the United States for the first time. They stayed in a hotel twenty minutes outside of Seoul. Before the decathlon, they were escorted on a pleasant sightseeing tour by Mr. Lee, and afterwards he took all of us out to a nice dinner. And during the decathlon, they had whooped and hollered for me through every event, congratulating me afterwards with tears in their eyes. Their love and support meant a lot.

We did have one crazy experience together after the competition. We were walking through the underground sidewalks that lead to shopping, and just for fun Sheri jumped out from behind a wall to scare her mom. So loud was her mom's shriek that five fully armed members of the Korean military immediately surrounded us with guns drawn. We were laughing at first, but then it took a little explaining to convince the soldiers we were just goofing off.

Since we'd all flown to Korea at different times, we had to take separate flights home. Sheri returned with the Seagram's group. My parents left on October 3, their wedding anniversary, and I was tickled to find out that the change in time zones actually extended their celebration by about twelve hours. As I sat in my window seat on the way back to Azusa, I felt relieved and happy. My first four-year Olympic cycle was over. And though I hadn't won, I'd done well and learned many valuable lessons for next time. I knew I'd be back.

■   ■   ■

Back in California, Sheri and I resumed our "normal" life. After her graduation from Azusa Pacific in May of 1988, she had started working as a neonatal intensive care nurse at the Children's Hospital in Los Angeles. I enjoyed seeing her pursue her career with an intensity not unlike my own with the decathlon.

Sheri and I had to deal with several pieces of difficult news after returning from the Games. First, Sheri's grandfather died suddenly, leaving us shocked and saddened. Then a week later, the owner of the duplex abruptly gave us six weeks' notice to move out. It was especially awkward because we were friends with the owner's family, and Sheri had been quite close to his daughter. Now we had to make some fast decisions. After pulling together all of our savings and writing lots of letters to the bank about my sponsorships, we managed to qualify for an FHA loan to buy a townhouse in nearby Montclair. The only problem was that it wouldn't be ready until February 1, and we were supposed to evacuate the duplex on January 1. So we ended up staying with the owner's daughter and her husband for the month of January. In spite of the stress and the strained friendships, I think the experience strengthened our marriage because it forced us to step out on our own and become more independent.

Another thing I did after returning from Seoul was write to my sponsors, Blublockers and Nike. I wanted them to know I was going for the '92 Olympic Games and that I still needed their support. I especially needed it now, since I'd made a decision to drop the job at Anheuser-Busch. The people there had been kind, and I was grateful to the company and to the Olympic Job Opportunity Program for the work. But I felt more and more like the association with a major beer manufacturer was a conflict of interest for me. At Coach Franson's urging, I'd begun speaking in schools and churches and to groups such as the Fellowship of Christian Athletes over the past few years, and I wanted my sponsorships to be as consistent as possible with my faith.

Of course that was easy to say when I had sponsors. But I soon found out that I'd have to scramble for more sponsors. Blublockers had suddenly decided to cut my funding significantly. Like a little kid asking his dad for more allowance, I practically begged them to keep up their support. I didn't know what else to do if I wanted to keep training. Fortunately, Nike had agreed to start sending me $500 a month after Seoul, which helped some, but still fell short of what I needed.

Securing sponsors took lots of hard work and persistence, I found, as well as business and marketing expertise that I didn't have. It was draining some of the emotional energy I needed for training. If I was going to get anywhere with the financial side of my career, I began to realize that I would need help.

At that time—early 1989—I was taking a biology class at Citrus College, a junior college right next to Azusa Pacific University. I hadn't forgotten about my education, and still wanted to graduate from APU and then work on my master's degree in family counseling. I had taken the biology class at Citrus because it was much cheaper and I could still transfer the credit back to APU. My professor, Terry Damron, and I were talking one day, and I mentioned that I was struggling to find sponsors.

"You sound like you need some help," he said. "Do you have a manager?"

No, I didn't—just a great coach.

"Well, maybe you should talk to my next-door neighbor," he said. "I think he might be able to help you out."

It seemed a little weird, but I was certainly willing to give it a try. My teacher walked me into his neighbor's backyard one afternoon and introduced us. His name was Bob Mendes, and with his partner, Mike Bone, he ran a sports marketing company in Monrovia called Pacific Sports Productions. Bob was friendly, and I sensed that he liked me as much as I liked him. A week later we made an appointment for breakfast.

I wanted to make a good first impression, so I wore the nicest shirt and tie I owned, both of which had a large U.S. Olympic Team logo. Since I didn't really have any other dressy clothes, I wore jeans to complete the outfit.

Bob and Mike probably chuckled under their breath when they first saw me that day at the Shilo restaurant. They listened as I described my background and my current situation with sponsors. As it turned out, their business was working with corporate clients to develop promotional opportunities within the sports world. Bob explained that they had absolutely no experience in representing athletes. That disappointed me, because I immediately liked both of them and wanted to work together. But I didn't give up, and apparently neither did they. Over the next few months we met several more times at the same restaurant. I never thought about it, but they told me later that I wore the same Olympic shirt and tie for every meeting. They must have wondered whether I owned any other clothes.

We had a good time together, though, and all three of us felt that we might be able to establish some kind of business relationship. None of us knew exactly what kind, however.

"Dave, we're willing to represent you," Bob said, "but we want you to know up front that we've never done this before."

"That's OK," I replied. "I've never had anyone represent me either, so let's do it and see what happens. We'll learn together."

They decided at first to simply help me out on a few of my contacts without signing a formal contract. For some reason, I still wanted to handle the Nike negotiations on my own.

At the same time, I continued training hard for the spring and summer season. My first meet would be the TAC Senior Championships on June 13–14—the day after my second wedding anniversary—and I wanted to be ready.

The competition took place in Houston, Texas, on two incredibly hot and humid days—evenings actually. Presumably the evening schedule would avoid the heat, but you never would have known it—the temperature stayed above 90 degrees. On top of the heat and humidity, the wind gusted unpredictably throughout, rendering many scores invalid for record purposes. I felt good and PR'd in the first two events, with a sub-eleven-second 100 meters and nearly 25 feet in the long jump. With each event that followed, I consistently logged in solid scores, and by the end of the first day I was in second place—a good position since my second day is stronger than that of most decathletes. I felt like I was having a great meet and that I'd probably win.

I didn't realize just how good a meet until late in the second day. Coach Franson had been checking the scoring tables and punching numbers into a calculator. After I ran a pretty fast hurdles, he had determined that I was actually on a pace to break Bruce Jenner's American record of 8634, scored at the 1976 Olympics. Coach didn't say anything to me at first; he didn't want to add any pressure. And although I sensed that something was stirring, I didn't ask, because I never check my score until just before the 1500.

Then I PR'd in the pole vault, clearing 16'10¾". I didn't know it, but with two events remaining, I was now *ahead* of pace for the American record. Coach Franson, keeping his cool, simply told me I was doing great and to keep it up. Behind the scenes, however, he could hardly contain his excitement.

Coach's roommate for the meet, decathlon guru Frank Zarnowski, actually ran to the phone to call his friend Bruce Jenner. There was no answer, but Frank left a message on his machine: "I'm at the TAC meet in Houston. If Dave Johnson throws a good javelin and runs 4:20 in the 1500 meters, he'll be the new American record holder."

Of course, I still didn't know what was going on, so I just stepped out to take my javelin throws. After two decent but not spectacular attempts, Coach decided he needed to talk to me. He told me I was very close to breaking the American record, and that I needed a javelin throw of about 228 feet to have a decent shot at it.

I was stunned, and needed a few seconds to catch my breath. Tears even welled up in my eyes as I realized that my dream of being one of the best was really coming true.

My final throw, however, was only 221 feet. I still had an outside chance at the record if I could run 4:18 or better in the 1500. My very best time to date was 4:28, and it would be extremely difficult to shave more than ten seconds off a PR—especially because the officials had divided the athletes into two heats rather than one. Several of the faster runners who would have helped me set the proper pace were in the first heat, and I basically ran alone in the second, managing only 4:31. Jenner's record would stand, at least for the time being. Even so, I ended up improving my PR by 300 points with a score of 8549.

I had not only won the meet and the U.S. championship, but I'd just posted the Number One score in the world. It blew me away to realize that if I had posted that score nine months earlier at the Olympic Games, I would have won. Coach Franson and I just looked at each other in amazement and gratitude. We knew that the Lord had brought us together for a very special reason. When I called Sheri that night and told her my score, she was so happy for me that she cried.

Zarnowski told me later that Jenner had called him back the day after the meet. "Whew!" Bruce said. "I checked the papers today and I didn't see that anyone broke my record!"

Actually, I had come a lot closer to it than people realized at first. Jenner's 8634 score had been with the old javelin. The new javelin, introduced in 1986, was designed to drop more quickly, resulting in shorter distances. Franson and Zarnowski calculated that if I'd thrown the old javelin, my score would be about 90 points higher, which would have equaled and possibly bettered Jenner's 8634. They both wrote letters explaining the situation to the records committee of The Athletics Congress.

My win in Houston qualified me to attend the World University Games in Duisberg, West Germany, followed by the annual meet in Talence, France. I had about seven weeks to train and prepare. During that period I sat down with Bob and Mike again, this time with the world's top score in my pocket. I think they realized I was serious in my quest to be the best, and that I had the potential to bring in some business for them as well, so we finally worked out a contract for Pacific Sports Productions to handle my sponsorships. Just to be sure, I had Sheri and Coach Franson meet them and give their approval before I signed. Bob and Mike still felt a little nervous about not being able to deliver sponsors, but we all agreed that it would be an adventure.

I should have let Pacific Sports handle the Nike account at this point, but I still felt like I was supposed to handle it on my own. They offered me a little more money—$250 more each month—but with something of a ho-hum attitude. I kept picking up from them that they really weren't interested in decathletes. I liked a lot of the people there, but at the corporate level they just didn't seem to care whether I was part of their team. Still, I hung on to the sponsorship for another year and hoped things would improve.

The World University Games were rainy and cold, but they did give me my first international win with a score of 8216. I enjoyed making friends from the other countries, especially Michael Medved of the Soviet Union. It was also nice to have Sheri fly out for the competition; she'd gotten a few days off work so she could join me. After the meet, the German Federation honored me with an invitation to put my footprint in cement alongside that of great German athletes such as

Jürgen Hingsen. They conducted a special ceremony there at the stadium.

From Germany, fellow American decathlete Sheldon Blockburger and I took the train to Talence, France, stopping in Monaco along the way to watch another international meet. Many of the French passengers complained because we had brought our vaulting poles on the train. Monaco was an awesome place—as beautiful as it had looked in the travel magazines. But again, our poles, which we'd left outside the tiny bungalow we slept in, seemed to pose a problem for the locals. Sheldon and I caught a few people playing with them and even throwing them into the trees. Neither one of us could figure out why.

The Meeting International D'Athlétisme in Talence was the same meet I'd done in 1986. It was fun to see some of the athletes I'd competed against in Seoul—Christian Plaziat, Daley Thompson, Mike Smith, and others. Christian, who was on his home turf, and Mike would be my primary competition.

Frank Zarnowski was serving as coach for the American delegation that year, and I enjoyed working with him for the first time. Frank is a passionate devotee of the decathlon who knows more about the sport than any living human being. I've told many people that he knows my career much better than I do, and it's true. He's been a great friend and a great support to me over the years. At this point, however, we were just getting to know each other.

I was pleased with my performance in the meet, even though I placed second behind Christian. It became obvious early in the first day, though, that there were irregularities in the officiating. Both Christian and I struggled in the long jump. I could only muster 23′7½″, way off my form, and Christian fouled on his first two attempts. On his last try, he stepped over the toeboard and fouled again, but the official overlooked it. Coach Zarnowski, a stickler for detail and for fairness, stormed out onto the track to protest. After inquiring about the officials, he discovered that the woman who ignored the foul just "happened" to be the mother of one of the other French decathletes!

Talk about a home field advantage. Unfortunately, nothing could be done. If the foul had been recorded he would have "no-marked" and effectively been eliminated from contention, but Christian's jump of more than 25 feet counted, giving him an extra hundred points or so.

I suppose I could have let the incident bother me, but for some reason I managed to let it go. Maybe all those lessons I'd been learning about focus were beginning to sink in. I simply needed to accept what had happened and move to the next event. I did get a little rankled the next day when the officials refused to approve my javelin for competition—the same one I'd been using legally all year. But I kept my anger under control and watched Frank fight it out with the officials.

In the end, Christian won by 77 points—8438 to 8361. It would have been great to beat him, because I would probably have earned a Number One ranking in the world. Instead, he got the win and the ranking. But I was proud of my score, my second best ever.

Back in the U.S., I was thrilled to learn that I'd been chosen as a finalist for the Jesse Owens award, given each year by The Athletics Congress to the person they consider to be the top American track athlete. It was the first time a decathlete had ever been nominated. They invited me and Sheri to their October convention in Washington, D.C., where the winner would be announced.

I didn't win. Roger Kingdom, two-time Olympic gold medalist and world-record hurdler, got the award instead, and it was well-deserved. But I got my own "award" at the convention which in many ways was just as satisfying. It came in the form of a news release from the TAC records committee:

> Move over, Bruce Jenner, you now share the American decathlon record with Dave Johnson of the New York [Athletic Club]. In the 1976 Olympic Games at Montreal, Jenner set a then world record and the current American record of 8,634 points while winning the gold medal and track immortality. However, Johnson scared that record when he won the decathlon title at

the USA/Mobil Championships in Houston last June with 8,549 points.

Johnson could have possibly broken Jenner's mark had he been throwing the same type of javelin Jenner had used in Montreal. In 1986 the IAAF, the world governing body for track and field, changed the specifications of the javelin to shorten the throwing distance of the implement for safety reasons.

At the General Meeting of TAC, the Records Committee felt that since Johnson was so close to the Jenner mark throwing a different javelin, he should also get credit. Thus Jenner will retain his American record with the notation "old javelin" beside it, while Johnson will also have the American record with the notation "new javelin."

Pretty cool. All the letters and computations from Coaches Franson and Zarnowski had paid off. It was an amazing feeling to be officially recognized for equaling a mark that had been virtually unchallenged for thirteen years. I was so thankful to both coaches, to The Athletics Congress for their gracious response, and most of all to God for inspiring me to victory.

What a year 1989 had been—U.S. champion, co-American record holder, World University Games champion, top score in the world. What in the world could be next?

■   ■   ■

The decathlon has always been a low-profile sport in the U.S.—way too low, if you ask me. Part of it is the inevitable result of its being an amateur sport without the benefit of organized and paid decathlon teams. You'll never see a Monday Night Decathlon on TV, for instance, with the Mississippi Masochists battling the Reno Robojocks. The decathlon simply doesn't work that way.

But very little was being done to promote or support the sport in America either. It rarely received national media coverage other than at the Olympics. Most corporations had no interest in sponsoring decathletes. Few high schools included the event at all, and only a handful of colleges, such as Mount

St. Mary's in Maryland, gave it the kind of attention that Azusa Pacific or Linn-Benton did. Even at national championship meets, attendance was dismal. For example, at the U.S. championships in which I recorded the world's highest score for 1989, there were often more officials on the track than spectators in the stands. Even today, decathlons seem to be purposely scheduled for the two days before a major track meet so that officials can test the facilities, equipment, and timing devices—sort of a "dry run" before the main event. Unfortunately, if something malfunctions or officiating procedures haven't been properly worked out, the decathletes may suffer.

All of these factors contributed to the relatively poor standing of American decathletes at the international level. No American had medaled in the Olympic games since Bruce Jenner's gold in 1976, and no American had been ranked Number One in the world since 1979. In fact, before I earned the Number Two ranking in 1989, only three other Americans had broken into the top ten on the world list during the 1980s.

A number of key people were working tirelessly to change that situation—Fred Samara, who'd been appointed 1992 Olympic coach, Harry Marra, track coach at San Francisco State, Mike Bozeman, Frank Zarnowski, and others. They'd been talking with various corporations and with the U.S. Olympic Committee for years to try to build a stronger support base for the decathlon. They envisioned a national program which would provide specialized training and mentoring for the country's top decathletes and prepare them for the Olympic Games.

As it turned out, the declaration of my 8549 score as a co-American record gave them another card to play. Potential decathlon sponsors began to take notice. For the first time in thirteen years, people were saying, the U.S. had an athlete as good as Bruce Jenner.

A major breakthrough occurred in early 1990 when John Bennett, senior vice president of VISA, combined with Fred and Harry to create the VISA Gold Medal Athlete Program. Designed exclusively for decathletes, the program had the full support and cooperation of the USOC and its Sports Science Division. VISA had been an Olympic sponsor since 1986, but this was the first time the corporation had zeroed in on one event. They agreed to sponsor a series of decathlon camps for the leading U.S. Olympic contenders, beginning with a three-day clinic at San Francisco State in April.

This represented a dramatic step forward for the decathlon in America. The sport was finally beginning to get the attention it deserved. And now I found myself in the position of leading this resurgence. VISA asked me to be an official spokesperson for the program, which would initially involve a six-city media tour with former gold medalist Bob Mathias, the program's honorary chairman.

Many things seemed to come together for me as a result of VISA's sponsorship. For the first time, I no longer felt like an isolated athlete struggling for recognition and support. Finally, here was a company that wanted me and other decathletes to be a part of their family, their team. And they didn't simply want me to represent their product—which I happily did—they wanted to help me become a better decathlete as well. I could hardly express how much it motivated me to have John Bennett and the others at VISA standing behind us in such a visible way. On top of all that, they paid me well enough that I no longer had to scramble to support Sheri and me. God had indeed been faithful and shown me that I could trust him with my decathlon dream.

It was an honor and a pleasure to travel with Bob Mathias, who I found to be not only a great person, but also a "regular guy." Facing the media so frequently was a new challenge for me, but after a while I got the hang of it. Coach Franson had been right a few years ago when he told me I'd need speaking skills someday.

The clinic was intense but impressive—even more so than my visits to the Olympic Training Center. In addition to the army of doctors and technicians, many of the top track and field coaches from around the country came to assist in the tests and training sessions. Best of all, four of the five living

American gold medalists—Mathias, Milt Campbell, Bill Toomey, and Bruce Jenner—joined us to share their experiences and advice. I was energized by the entire experience.

This was the first time I'd ever met Bruce, and I felt awkward, but he was friendly and we got along well. It amazed me to think that this was the man Coach Bakley had told me about during that first phone call eight years ago. I never would have thought that now I'd be sharing the American decathlon record with him.

Altogether seventeen decathletes attended the clinic, including one guy I'd been hearing more and more about lately: Dan O'Brien. He'd been hampered by injuries on and off since the '88 Trials, but recently he'd been improving significantly. The rumor was that he was fast and had lots of natural ability.

Although this was the first time I'd really met Dan, I'd interacted with him briefly by phone a couple of months prior to the clinic. I'd gotten a call from his high school coach, who was helping Dan with some of his training. The coach was a Christian, and thought that it might be good for Dan to hang around and train with a Christian decathlete. Would it be possible for Dan to come down to Southern California and train with me for a few months?

I didn't quite know what to say. I knew how beneficial it had been for me to train in a Christian environment. But I also knew I'd been traveling a lot and that I needed to carve out more time in my schedule for Sheri. Plus I was already training with several other guys. So, unaware of what the future held for Dan and me, I had politely declined.

A few weeks later, Dan had phoned me personally. "I know my coach called you," he said, "but I was just wondering if you could give me a little help finding a shoe sponsor."

I gave him some names and numbers from my list of contacts, and then we chatted for a few minutes. He seemed like a nice guy to me.

As I watched Dan during the clinic I could see that he truly had exceptional talent. If he stayed healthy, there was no question he'd be a serious Olympic contender. At the end of the camp, we all said goodbye to each other until the U.S. Championships in June.

Dan looked at me before he left and said, "Dave, watch out—I'm coming."

That's a pretty bold statement, I thought.

"Yeah, I know you are," I quickly replied, "and I hope you do."

Two months later, he did—at the U.S. championships at Cerritos College in Norwalk, California. This year the meet fell exactly on Sheri's and my third anniversary, and I had arranged ahead of time to have a rose sent up to her in the stands. I had trained hard and I was ready, but I hadn't planned for this to be the year's "big meet." I was looking ahead to the Goodwill Games in July. The warm, sunny weather and a slightly over-limit wind set the stage for some high scores. From the crack of the opening gun, Dan made it clear that he meant business. He ran the 100 in 10.40, the second-fastest decathlon 100 in history. I was behind him with a 10.78, still a PR for me.

I had an excellent first day, PRing in three events—the 100, the shot put, and the high jump. But Dan was having an incredible day. He PR'd in the 100, and then broke the world decathlon record in the long jump with a distance of 26'4½". To give you an idea of just how well we were doing, at the end of five events I was *ahead* of the pace that earned me the American record last year. But I was *trailing* Dan by nearly 300 points. I was amazed at the high score he had racked up.

Again, I had to play catch-up on the second day, something I'd done many times. But I loved the competition and rose to the occasion. After the hurdles, Dan's lead had increased to 339 points. I had four events left to make up the difference.

Fortunately, they were my strongest events. I thought I'd grabbed 200 of those points back when I outthrew Dan in the discus by more than thirty feet. But on his last effort, he came up just seven feet short of my throw, and I'd only gained 50.

The pole vault marked the major turning point, however: Dan could only manage 14'1¼", while I cleared 16'4¾", hacking 208 points off of his lead. Then in the javelin, my best and favorite event, I heaved about 35 feet further than Dan and took the lead by 65 points.

Up till now I'd been looking more at the points I needed to make up; I hadn't been paying much attention to my overall score. But by the time I finished the 1500, it hit me that I'd just amassed 8600 points, the second highest score in American history. Dan had faded in the last event, but still ended up in second with a PR of 8483—the third all-time highest.

The Dan and Dave rivalry was born. I loved it.

Afterwards, the atmosphere was jubilant as Dan and I met the press together, boasting and joking with each other. "Some jaws are going to drop in Europe when they see these scores," I said. "The decathlon is back in the U.S.!"

When Dan predicted that he'd still improve, I knew he was right, but I couldn't help ribbing him a little: I smiled and said that the only way he'd beat me in Barcelona was by topping 9000.

Of course, we'd have plenty of chances to compete between now and Barcelona—starting with the second Goodwill Games the following month. Jointly sponsored by the U.S. and the then-U.S.S.R., the affair comes closer than any international competition to the feel of the Olympic Games. Many sports are represented in addition to track and field. TV cameras move in. And as in the Olympics, gold, silver, and bronze medals are awarded in front of thousands of spectators.

This year the Goodwill Games decathlon took place at the University of Washington in Seattle. My Soviet friend Michael Medved was there. I definitely wanted to beat Dan, but more than that I wanted to show the world that American decathletes were now a force to be reckoned with.

The conditions in Husky Stadium fit all those of a typical Northwest day: cooler than usual in the low 60s, breezy, though still legal, and a period of rain on the second day. In many ways the meet proceeded similarly to the last one: Dan quickly seized the lead and held on tight. The large, friendly crowd added lots of energy and excitement to the competition, especially during the high jump. Performance-wise, it was a standard first day for me—solid but unspectacular except for a 48.41 PR in the 400. Once again, I was nearly 300 points behind Dan after five events.

He and I both knew what the second day would be like— it would come down to the last three events. Back at the hotel after Day One, Dan asked me about the two events that were my best and, at that time, his worst. He wanted to know if I got scared before the pole vault and the javelin, and how I handled it. I told him that my confidence had basically come from years of experience, and that his confidence would grow as well.

The next day, after seven events I remained more than 300 points out of the lead. In the vault, I didn't jump nearly as high as I'd hoped, but still managed to reclaim nearly 200 points from Dan. Then, with my first javelin throw, I grabbed the lead for the first time. It lasted for only a few minutes until Dan snatched it back with a much shorter throw that still gave him enough points to stay ahead. My final throw was a PR of 225'3", which pulled me within 23 points of first place with one event left.

I thought I'd probably beat Dan in the 1500, but didn't feel the same assurance of victory that I'd felt on other occasions. This one was too close for comfort. Coach Franson had figured out that I needed to run three seconds faster than Dan in order to win. As we lined up to begin, I prayed, *Lord, I'm going to run my very best and leave the rest up to you. I'll be an example for you even if I end up in second.*

For the first two laps, it was anybody's call. Dan, Canadian Mike Smith, Soviet Roman Terechov, and I packed together and stayed out in the lead. Then, on lap three, Dan drifted back just a little, then a little more, until I knew I'd won the gold. My time was 4:26.19, nearly ten seconds ahead of him. Final score: Johnson, 8403; O'Brien, 8358.

Man—this was the decathlon at its best. Afterwards I praised just about everything except the weather: Dan for his powerful performance, VISA for their sponsorship, the USOC and TAC for their decathlon support, and God for giving me my purpose and helping me to be a good role model.

The VISA people were thrilled that their main spokesperson had won the U.S. championship, the Goodwill Games, and had posted the highest score in the world for the second straight year. They also applauded the fact that Dan, a beneficiary of their training camp, had burst so quickly and powerfully onto the world scene. Our strong showing, combined with the excellent response to their clinic, inspired them to take a further step of commitment to America's decathletes. In late fall of 1990, John Bennett announced that VISA would be forming and sponsoring a U.S. Decathlon Team in order to help America reclaim the Olympic gold medal and the title of "World's Greatest Athlete."

The program would focus primarily on training and financially supporting the top ten decathletes in the U.S.—the "elite decathletes," as they're called—who would comprise the team. Intensive week-long training camps would take place twice a year and would include the team itself, past Olympic gold medalists, and an additional twenty-five up-and-coming decathletes. It was an amazing development, one that I believe will result in top world-ranked American decathletes well into the next century.

VISA's sponsorship was unprecedented in the sport of track and field. As Frank Zarnowski explained, it was "the first of its kind to provide exclusive financial assistance from one corporation to train and support athletes competing in a single event." I called it incredible.

Speaking of sponsors, Mike and Bob at Pacific Sports had been working hard to line up companies that would sponsor me individually. Earlier in the year they had ended the Blublockers contract and signed me up with Oakley sunglasses, who provided a modest monthly stipend plus a great supply of the coolest glasses I'd ever seen through.

In the fall, my contract with Nike came up for renewal. For the past year I'd been wearing their jersey and their shoes, and they'd been sending me $750 a month. I appreciated the money, but I still got the impression that they tended to prefer sprinters and distance runners to decathletes. After the Goodwill Games, they offered to renew the contract at $1,000 a month plus various incentives, but I still felt uncomfortable about our relationship, so I finally turned over the contract to Mike and Bob.

Meanwhile, they'd been quietly approaching other shoe companies, including Reebok. I'd made contact with them earlier in the year through former Olympic decathlete and world record holder Russ Hodge. I first met Russ, a neat Christian guy, at a prayer breakfast, and we'd become good friends over the years. Russ knew someone at Reebok, and agreed to send them a letter on my behalf. So my name had been on their desk before, but I hadn't gotten much of a response because of my ties to Nike.

Then, a senior sports marketing director at Reebok, Chester Wheeler, saw my picture in a *GQ* magazine photo spread that featured several Olympic athletes. He had been looking for an athlete to help them promote a new line of cross-training shoes and draw some attention to Reebok's new sponsorship with the USOC and the 1992 Olympics. An Olympic decathlete seemed a natural choice. He called Jim Millman of Millsport, VISA's sports marketing agency, wondering about my availability. Jim had been one of the key figures in creating the VISA Gold Medal Program. I was under contract with Nike, he told Chester, but not particularly happy with the relationship.

The very next day, Saturday, Chester called Mike Bone to ask about me. He immediately sent a bunch of shoes for me to try out, and arranged to meet with us the following week. We were all excited. It seemed as if something big was in the works.

When Bob and Mike and I sat down with him a few days later, I showed my eagerness to talk by wearing a pair of the new Reeboks with my suit. (Yes, I had finally gone out and bought a decent suit.) I liked Chester right away—his down-to-earth style, his sincerity, his enthusiasm. I could tell that I'd enjoy working with him and with Reebok.

Discussions went on between Pacific Sports and both Reebok and Nike through the summer and into the fall. Again and again the bottom line seemed to be that Reebok really cared about me as a person and an athlete, while to Nike I was just another promising athlete wearing their shoes.

In late fall, at about the same time that all the VISA news was breaking, Mike, Bob and I traveled to Seattle for the annual TAC convention. I'd been nominated a second time for the Jesse Owens award, so I'd have to sit nervously through an awards dinner with the other four finalists to find out if I won. I didn't. But we had meetings scheduled with both Nike and Reebok.

The Nike meeting went pretty much as expected—friendly, but uninspiring. Reebok, on the other hand, had decided to make its move. They offered me a three-year contract and more than twice as much money as Nike, along with a host of incentives. They also said they were thinking about using me in a TV commercial.

At one point in the breakfast, Mike had asked Chester about how I'd fit into their promotional plans.

Chester looked right at me and said, "Dave, we believe you are the world's greatest cross trainer, and we intend to promote you as such. You will be Reebok's Bo Jackson."

Whoa, I thought, *where do I sign?*

That same day I taped a short video introducing myself to the Reebok employees, to be shown at their national convention. And within a few weeks, they brought me to their home office in Stoughton, Massachusetts, for a number of fun promotional projects. I met a lot of great people, including the president, Paul Fireman.

There was one other thing Chester had mentioned at that breakfast meeting. He said that Reebok also intended to sign on Dan as a backup in case something happened to me before the 1992 Olympics. They envisioned me taking Reebok through the '92 Games and a gold medal, and then I'd pass on the mantle to Dan for '96.

It all felt like it was meant to be. VISA was providing me with valuable training and support which made me feel like part of a team. And now Reebok was making me feel like part of a family. Pacific Sports had negotiated two major contracts that would provide quite a substantial income for me. These sponsors, combined with the support of my wife and my Azusa family, spurred me to train and work even harder as a decathlete. They also gave me further confirmation that God was taking care of me and making it possible to be a role model for him in the sports world.

Pole vault

PR: 17'3¾"

This is the only event in which you use something other than your body—a fiberglass pole—to create force.

It's also the only event that can literally kill you.

Many years of practice are needed to develop the proficiency and confidence to vault consistently. It is clearly the most technical event of the decathlon—and the most dangerous. The physical strength and the mental concentration it requires is awesome.

You begin by carrying the pole and running like a madman, which is exactly what you must be to even try this event. As you reach the bar, which is perched somewhere in the stratosphere, you must suddenly plant the pole in a metal box and drive all your speed and force into it until it bends precariously. You then rock upward, lifting your feet together as the pole begins to straighten. When you're completely upside down (looking back down the runway) and the pole is almost fully extended, you quickly pull up with your arms, rotate toward the bar, and push off the pole in one smooth motion. At this point you'll actually see the bar for the first time. Adjust your position, raise your arms so they don't catch the bar, and you're over.

That's if everything goes right. And in the pole vault, there are many things that can go wrong. If you don't have enough speed, or if you plant too early or too late or too out of line, that pole will turn against you. It may refuse to bend, or it may bend too much and snap, or it may fling you in any direction except toward the protective mat. You could easily miss the pit, land on your head, break your neck, or suffer many other injuries.

Probably the vaulter's greatest fear is breaking a pole. The pain in your hands from the vibration is incredible, worse than when you break a baseball bat. You could get fiberglass splinters, and you may be poked or scraped, or even impaled, by flying pieces of the pole. And most terrifying of all, you have no idea where you'll land and what part of your body you'll land on.

But it's an awesome feeling when your body becomes part of the pole and you simply soar through the air. When you're really "on," vaulting is the most fun and exhilarating of all the events.

What does the pole vault represent for me? Many of the same things as the other bar event, the high jump. You have an identifiable goal that you know ahead of time, and you're able to reach it in steps rather than all at once. But there are two distinctives. First, the goal I must reach is dramatically higher, almost beyond imagination. I'm even more tempted to give up and go home without even trying.

The second distinctive is both a gift and a challenge. I don't have to clear that bar completely on my own. It's not all up to me. I am given a powerful, valuable resource—the pole—to help me reach my goal. If I treat that pole with respect, handle it properly, and tap all of its potential, I can sail to incredible heights. If I don't, it becomes a burden, weighing me down when my goal is to clear the bar.

We all face certain tasks or problems that challenge us to draw upon our inner resources. But the pole vault reminds me of the huge, overwhelming goals that seem humanly unachievable. When those situations arise, we can always believe that God will provide some kind of resource to help us reach that goal. It might be people, money, time, or whatever will give us the help we need. If we remember to treat those resources with dignity and manage them wisely, we'll accomplish things we never dreamed possible.

■ ■ ■

▪ chapter nine ▪

WHO IS THE WORLD'S GREATEST ATHLETE?

IN THE YEARS between the Seoul and the Barcelona Olympic Games, my schedule had grown increasingly hectic. Big meets, sponsor commitments, and a growing number of speaking engagements often required me to travel. And because I had set my sights on winning the Games in 1992, I had stepped up my training regimen. All of these changes caused stress in my relationship with Sheri. It seemed I wasn't home much, and when I was, I felt too tired or too preoccupied with the decathlon to be there for her. I was so focused on being the best in the world that I didn't set aside regular time to enjoy and build our relationship. When she complained, I tried to communicate the importance of lengthy training schedules, keeping my sponsors happy, and so on, but inside I knew she was right. Actually, we probably had more time together than most couples, but while I was physically present, my mind was usually still out on the track.

Slowly we were learning to accept what the decathlon was doing to our lives and trying to make adjustments to preserve and strengthen our marriage. It wasn't easy, and the process continues today. What made it so difficult was my belief that I'd been *called* to the decathlon by God, that it was, at the time, the vehicle through which I served him. He had given me this athletic ability, and I wanted to give it back to him by doing my very best in competition. That required me to make certain sacrifices.

On the other hand, I also felt called to love and care for Sheri. Our situation was probably similar to that of many who feel called to "full-time Christian service." They do what they believe God wants them to do, and they love their spouses and children, but family responsibilities often take a distant second place to the "ministry." I didn't believe God wanted it that way. If I focused so much on doing God's will that I ignored the people who meant the most to me, then I wasn't doing God's will. So I'd been challenged again and again to balance my calling to the decathlon with my calling to my wife.

We both had to adapt. For instance, Sheri thought at first that I was ignoring her during the week or two before a big meet, or if I didn't pay attention to her at the meet itself. She had to learn that it was part of my preparation to become much more focused during those times. Of course, I'd drop everything if an emergency arose, but otherwise I wasn't very available emotionally. During a meet, I just knew that in order to give one hundred percent of myself, I had to give 100 percent of my attention to the task before me. It was a long time before she began to understand that I couldn't give her more than an occasional smile from the track until after the meet ended. For out-of-town meets, we even had separate hotel rooms. I'd travel ahead of time, and she'd arrange to stay in a different room in the same hotel when she arrived. As soon as the meet is over, she'd move in with me.

On my side, I had to learn to be more sensitive to Sheri's needs. I would try to block out time just to be with her, and when we were together I tried to listen more to her feelings and let her see mine. After a big meet I reminded myself that I had been largely unavailable to her, and that I now needed to be *extra* available because she would have plenty of things that she'd been saving up to talk about. As much as possible, I tried to let go of the intense focus after I trained so I could be more present when I get home. In a way, it was a lesson I learned from the decathlon: Just as I needed to put each event behind me and shift my focus to the next one, I also needed to let go of the decathlon itself after I trained or after a meet so I could focus on Sheri and the other parts of my life.

The struggle to have children had been another difficult aspect of our marriage. Sheri had wanted to have children since as far back as she could remember. We had stopped using birth control after the Seoul Games, but without immediate results. Then in early 1989 she got pregnant but miscarried within a few weeks. It would not be her last miscarriage, we would later discover. Each time her period came, her frustration grew at not being able to get pregnant. She felt that something was wrong with her, that she could not be complete as a woman until she had her own child. Unfortunately, I wasn't much of a support to her. I told her that I definitely wanted to have children, but that I felt they would come only when it was time. What I realized later was that she really needed for me just to try to understand and to empathize with her needs.

Starting in 1991 I began writing down some of my thoughts in journal form on a computer. One entry especially, seemed to sum up many of the feelings I had about Sheri and about my life at that time:

> Having Sheri as my wife is the best thing I have ever done. She has helped me realize the four main focuses in my life: First, I must grow as a Christian. Second, I must take care of my relationship with my wife. Third, I must perfect the ministry that God has chosen for me—the decathlon. Fourth, I must work on my future ministry as a sports psychologist, public speaker, coach, teacher, or whatever God calls me to. That's it! Life seems so much easier to grasp and control. Even though things are not perfect, I know that God has it all under control and will take care of things his way, not mine. My job is to do my very best in all that I do. It doesn't mean I don't have a killer instinct. I do! It's a killer instinct to show people God's power and his love in the way I compete, so that maybe through me someone might come to know him.

> Without an incredible woman by my side supporting me through all of this and helping me take my goals in the right

direction, I would not be doing very well. And without her, there would have been and there will be no Olympic Games for David Johnson. One of the key things that makes someone the best is the people who are in his life.

■ ■ ■

The ink had barely dried on the Reebok contract when they began following up on their promises. They slated me to do a TV commercial for their new Pump Reebok line of cross-training shoes, and they wanted it to compete directly with the Nike cross-trainers endorsed by Bo Jackson. So in my first major commercial, I'd have to beat up on my former sponsor. It was all in good fun.

I'd had a little bit of previous experience with commercials. During the past few years I had put my name in with a local talent agency and made a few dollars here and there as an extra in various sports-related TV ads. Once I had to roll around on the track and get dirty for a Gatorade spot. Another time I hurdled over the camera for a European sports drink. And I'd actually had the principal action part in 1988 for Seagram's "Send the Families" commercial. An actor looked into the camera and said all the lines, but I played his double and did several of the decathlon events. I was hired because they needed someone with track skills; little did they know that I would be going to Seoul and that Sheri would benefit from their program.

But I'd never been the lone character and speaker in any kind of ad, so I was pretty nervous as we prepared to film the Reebok commercial in February of 1991. My lines, which I read from a prompter, went like this: "Hi, I'm Dave Johnson. For my training for the 1992 decathlon, I switched to the Pump from Reebok. When I'm pumped up, my feet have support, protection, and a custom fit for leaping, vaulting, spinning, jumping, sprinting, hurdling, racing, running, throwing, and uh, shot putting! Now, *I'm* the guy who knows about cross-training. Pump up—[then I toss the Nike shoe]—and air out." That thirty-second commercial may have looked simple on the TV screen, but it took six long hours to shoot. I was amazed at how many takes it took to get it just right, and how they changed the backgrounds and moved things around. But I liked the way it turned out.

By this time my financial situation had improved dramatically. Additional sponsors signed on, such as Hinckley & Schmitt bottled water, and Body Fuel, an electrolyte drink similar to Gatorade. A lot more money began coming in—more than I'd ever seen in my life. Sheri and I had been able to buy a house, and it was now getting to the point where she didn't need to work at the hospital any more. But she loved her job and wanted to continue. I just felt thankful that God was providing for us in such a wonderful way.

Shortly after these big sponsor contracts were signed, I realized that money considerations could become a major distraction for me. I guess it works both ways: When I didn't have enough money to live on a few years ago, I obsessed over how to find some. Now, with a lot of money coming in, I discovered I could obsess about it just as much. My contracts usually provided for a base amount of money that I received each month, plus a myriad of bonuses or incentives tied to my performance. I might receive a bonus for winning a meet, for winning the U.S. championship, for setting a world record, for attaining a certain ranking, and so on. These incentives were good if they spurred me to keep improving, but the whole concept of bonuses could backfire if I thought about it too much. If I always stopped before or during a meet to ponder the financial implications of reaching (or not reaching) a certain score, I'd go crazy. It'd be impossible to focus.

So I decided not to think about how much I was making. That was never my purpose for doing the decathlon anyway. Sure I wanted to make money, but I didn't feel the need or the desire to become a sports tycoon. I just wanted to be able to live comfortably, take care of my family, and know that there was money in the bank if I needed it. I always reviewed the contracts to make sure I was getting paid what I was worth, and to be sure I could fulfill my side of the deal, but then I honestly tried to forget about it. That way I could focus on being that same ol' Dave, curious about the athletic ability that the Lord had given him, who wanted to go out there on the track, putting himself on the line for God and seeing what came out of it.

Between training, sponsor work, speaking, and a couple of meets, the spring went by quickly. VISA sponsored another camp in early April—the first one since they had created the USA/VISA Decathlon Team—and it was conducted right at Azusa Pacific University. Coach Franson served as host, and once more it really motivated me to work hard and improve my events. Dan was there too, and from his performances I could see that he would be even tougher to beat this year. He too had recently signed up with Reebok, so we would both be "working" for the same company.

At the end of the camp, Dan came up to me and said goodbye again. He had the same look on his face as he had last year when he had told me to watch out. But for some reason, this time he didn't say anything other than "see you later." Maybe he'd decided to let his body and his performance do the talking.

Later that month, I did my first decathlon wearing a Reebok jersey—the Mt. SAC Relays, hosted by APU. All went quite smoothly and I won easily with a score of 8267. Mt. SAC was more of a practice meet for me, mainly because I was looking ahead to the U.S. Championships in New York. Placing in the top three there would qualify me for the World Championships in Tokyo at the end of August. My goal for New York was first to make the World team and then to win the meet. I was hoping to peak in Tokyo with a win and possibly a world decathlon record.

As the U.S. meet drew closer, my intensity level rose, which was normal. But perhaps it was a little higher because I knew I'd be facing Dan for the first time this season. I'd beat him twice last year, but he posed the most serious threat yet to the national title I'd held for two years.

An incident during a game of golf with my friend Kevin Reid showed me just how "on edge" I was. Some guy from the group behind us had hit his ball up onto the green just as we were stepping off. He did yell "fore," but I still thought he should have waited a little longer before hitting. I yelled at him, he yelled back, and I just had torn off my shirt and started to go after him when he apologized. The pressure had vented itself without warning. But I didn't want it to be directed at other people; I wanted to control it until the meet and then allow it to explode into a stellar performance.

I flew to New York City a few days ahead of time to get settled and check out the meet location—Downing Stadium on Randalls Island, right in the middle of the East River. Kevin, who'd been hired by Coach Franson as an assistant coach, came along to work with me. We stayed at a nice hotel in Times Square and lifted weights at the New York Athletic Club. I needed to distract myself from fretting about the meet, so Kevin and I goofed off and explored the city—beginning with our hotel. Just for fun, we walked up a few extra flights of stairs one night and came out on a floor that was still under construction. Pushing open another door, we emerged into a section of the building completely exposed to the outdoors— nothing but concrete and steel. What a great discovery. We climbed girders in the stale night air until we found a good perch to enjoy the view and listen to the blaring horns and car alarms. It was the perfect distraction.

We got up early on June 12—my fourth wedding anniversary—for the first day of the meet. Sheri, her mom, and my mom had flown in the night before; I would see them briefly at the stadium. When we arrived there, workmen were still scurrying around getting the subpar facility in shape. They were actually pouring a new runway for the long jump pit on the morning of the meet, even though a new surface needs a week to cure before it can be used. Coach Franson had even grabbed a shovel and gone over to help.

At 11 a.m., under sunny skies, the gun went off to start the 100 meters. Dan and I were in the same heat, and he burned up the track in 10.23, the fastest time ever recorded for a decathlon 100. Unfortunately—and inexcusably—officials had forgotten to bring a wind gauge, which negated the time for record purposes. I ran a healthy 10.87, though it seemed slow compared to Dan. It looked like we were in for a high-scoring meet.

Not surprisingly, the new long jump runway surface had not set in time, so we had to use the dilapidated old pit. I managed a decent leap of 24'¾", but Dan sailed more than two feet farther, racking up more than 1000 points for the second straight event. Then I PR'd in the shot put, only to watch Dan outthrow me by three feet for his own PR. Clouds had moved in and drenched us with rain for the high jump, again won by Dan.

By the end of the 400, Dan had set a new world record for a first-day score—a whopping 4747. I was in second with 4269, an excellent score, but nearly 500 points behind.

It would take nothing short of a herculean effort to catch him this time. On the second day, his lead increased to nearly 750 points by the end of the pole vault. Even after strong PRs in the javelin and the 1500, I was only able to reclaim about 300 of those points. Dan's final score? 8844, only three points short of Daley Thompson's world record. And mine? 8467, which was my third best ever, but in my mind paled next to Dan's.

Dan had blown me off the island.

Actually, I'd had a fine, consistent meet. Other than Dan, my closest competitor was 350 points behind. And I'd made the world championship team, the primary goal I'd set for this meet. But I still felt as if I'd lost. To me, I hadn't placed second—I'd been beaten. Bad. "I don't think I was ready to score 8800 points in that meet," I later wrote in my computer journal. "Dan was. I can't wait to have a meet like he did."

I tried to forget about it that night after the meet. Sheri and I celebrated our anniversary and stayed together in my hotel room. Then she and her mom took off on a side trip, and Kevin and I went home.

A few weeks later, I had a short out-of-town speaking engagement. When I returned home late at night and opened the front door, I walked into a pair of balloons—one pink and one blue—tied to the knob. Sheri, who'd been lying on the couch waiting for me, sat up and smiled.

I didn't get it.

"What are these?" I said, looking at the balloons. "Did you just go to a baby shower?"

"No, Dave!" she said, exasperated. "I'm pregnant—we're gonna have a baby!"

Whoa. Surprise. I stood there in shock for a minute. Then I gave her a big hug and a kiss, and sat down on the couch as she told me how she'd found out and what the doctor had said. She'd felt queasy over the past few weeks and gotten sick a few times, but didn't say anything about it. When she realized her period was late, she had taken a do-it-yourself preganancy test twice. The results, however, were negative. She was confused, because she had all the symptoms of pregnancy.

Finally, her doctor had taken a blood test and determined that she was indeed pregnant. He had expressed concern about the stability of the child, however, and had prescribed proges-terone shots as a precaution. She'd need an injection every day until her eleventh or twelfth week.

Whew. This was one of those situations where my focus on the decathlon conflicted with my genuine desire to be there for Sheri. I was happy for her and for us, but I was concentrat-ing so much of my mental energy on training for the World Championships—and dealing with my "loss" to Dan—that it was hard for me to show a lot of excitement. But I tried to help her out a little more over the summer since she often felt lousy, and often got up with her in the middle of the night when she'd have a case of the heaves.

Meanwhile, I'd been logging in some solid workouts. I knew I needed a sudden and dramatic improvement in my performance if I wanted to outscore Dan in Tokyo, though, and it wasn't happening. I grew discouraged. On July 15, I wrote down these thoughts:

> Training is going well, but I feel like my events are staying the same instead of getting better and it seems to be bothering me. I feel impatient and almost helpless. I'm not satisfied with what

God is allowing me to do. In the past I have always trusted that God knew what is best. Through good times and bad I have trusted that the Lord was going to get me through it. I can't stop trusting him now. The decathlon has developed to a point that has become the most challenging and competitive thing that I will ever do with my life. It is getting all of the attention I always wished that it had. Am I really up for the challenge? All the anxiety built up inside me (from worrying about OB [O'Brien] scoring so many points) has started to make me feel depressed. It makes me feel inadequate. It makes me feel that the challenge is too great. That my skills will never develop to that level. Or is it that I am afraid of the pain, the actual bodily pain that I will go through in the meet that brings me to that level? . . . I guess this entry marks the desire to completely release whatever I am feeling. I'm going to try to just "let it flow" naturally, while not concerning myself with making sense of it all.

On the very day of that entry, I began having trouble with my left knee. I had first noticed slight pain a week and a half earlier, but now it hurt a lot. Three days later I attempted to compete in the Olympic Festival at UCLA, but I had to drop out after the 100 because the knee was bothering me too much. I certainly didn't want to make it worse and miss Tokyo.

The doctors said that I had strained a calf attachment area in my knee. It was weird: I had no trouble vaulting, throwing, high jumping, even running the 1500. I only felt pain when I sprinted. So I continued training in the non-sprinting events and it seemed to get a little better.

I also began to sort out why I'd gotten depressed after Dan beat me. I'd allowed myself to become sidetracked from my central purpose. Here's how I explained it in my journal:

Earlier I was complaining that I felt inadequate and sick. It was because I was losing the eye of the tiger. I was taking things for granted. I was forgetting that the way to succeed is to give it everything you've got. Be thankful for the talent that God has given you, get excited and go for it. I guess I sort of needed to have the decathlon taken away from me in order to really see how important it is to me. I lost the edge because I was afraid of losing. "If I'm going to lose, why even try" has been my attitude. That's a bad attitude when I have just as much chance to win as anyone.

With the World Championships only a month away, my knee was receiving daily ultrasound and acuscope treatments and began to improve. It still hurt at the end of each day, and was far from healed, but I got in some good workouts on it. I was able to do some sprinting and hurdling during the first week of August, which felt like progress. I needed to have a healthy knee if I was to do well in Tokyo, and I hoped that by God's grace it would get better. If it didn't, I would have to accept that it wasn't my time yet. I would trust that God had a plan for me and that I'd know what it was soon.

My journal entries during that first week of August capture a lot of what was running through my head:

8/2/91 My attitude and my self-worth are improving. I must continue to have a positive attitude. Think only positive about myself and my chances of doing well. OB [Dan] is doing his first day of a decathlon in Spain today. I hope everything goes well for him. I think the meet he is doing is too close to the World Championships; he may not have enough recovery time with all the travel. We definitely will see if he can score high again.

8/6/91 I think I'm ready to do well. But just thinking it won't make it reality—I've got to *make* it happen. I found out that OB didn't do the decathlon in Spain. He did a few events in the open meet—something I wanted to do but wasn't invited. He did very well, throwing 172 in the discus and vaulting 17'2". He also ran a 48.2 in the 400 and hurdled around 13.90. He is a stud! I still think that I can beat him if we both have a great meet. It feels like I have more hidden points than he does. I just pray that some day I get to blast a big one. If I can muster 8700 points in Japan, I will be in the medals, maybe even win the whole thing. I'm capable of it without any PRs.

But I've got to remember that no one really cares anyway. No one cares what you score but you—and maybe Frank Zarnowski. A few years down the road no one will care. The decathlon is a special thing that God is allowing me to do. No one will get more from it than me. So when it comes down to it, I need to just go out there and concentrate on doing my best. Get the meet out of the way, add up the points, and give the credit to God, because he gave me the talent and the mind to be there. That's it—think nothing else. Think nothing but positive thoughts.

The week before I left for Tokyo, I went to the doctor with Sheri. They did an ultrasound and I was able to watch the image of the baby moving around. I had already heard the heartbeat, but to actually see the baby's movements got me excited about being a father. I couldn't wait to have our own little kid romping around the house. Because of all the hormones she'd been taking, poor Sheri had been throwing up left and right for the past two months. The very sight of the kitchen sink would send her running into the bathroom. We had decided that she'd be better off not traveling to Japan. Instead, she left that day to stay with her parents in Sweet Home, Oregon, until I returned.

I bombed in Tokyo.

Or rather, I couldn't get through the meet and had to drop out. My knee had acted up again a few days beforehand, and gave me too much pain to be competitive. From the moment I took off in the 100 I knew my knee wouldn't last, so I simply tried to hang on as long as I could. It rained for most of the two days, which further dampened my spirits. There was great TV coverage here in the States, and it seemed like the whole world was watching as I limped around the track in the 400, every step searingly painful. Coach said it was the most courageous thing I'd ever done. Altogether I completed seven events with subpar scores, then no-heighted in the pole vault, then threw a strong javelin before withdrawing. Todd Christiansen of NBC and a few other reporters interviewed me afterwards. But the big story, of course, was Dan O'Brien's huge win with a score of 8812. Mike Smith of Canada took second with 8549, and Christian Schenk of West Germany third with 8394.

An interesting thing had happened on the first day, though, just after the high jump. Dan had not yet taken a commanding lead, and the meet was still up for grabs. But he struggled in the high jump and could only clear 6'3¼", way under his PR of nearly seven feet. As I stood nearby, I could see the distress in his face; he thought he'd blown the meet for sure. His coaches, Mike Keller and Rick Sloan, were trying to reassure him.

At first I wanted to turn and walk away; I was feeling so low myself that I didn't have much to offer anyone else. Then I think the Lord told me to help.

"Hey, it's OK, Dan," I said to him. "No one did very well in the high jump anyway. From what I can tell, there's no one out here who can beat you. Why don't you go out and prove it with your last six events?"

Maybe he figured I'd been around long enough to know what I was talking about. I could see his confidence returning. Even though I was dealing with my own disappointment, it was neat to watch Dan bounce back and beat everyone. Perhaps the Lord gave me that opportunity as a reminder that Dan was not so much my adversary, but a gifted teammate and friend who needed my support.

■   ■   ■

After all the ups and downs of the summer—mostly downs—I looked forward to life getting back to normal at home. Sheri and I would finally be able to have more time together, and we could begin preparing the house and ourselves for the baby's arrival. Thankfully, her constant throwing up had ended as she no longer had to take the hormone shots. She was even starting to show a little bit, and happily began to wear some of her maternity clothes.

On Monday, September 16, she felt the baby kick for the first time. I was out training and had arranged to meet her at former Azusa teammate Jack Nance's house to watch Monday Night Football with a bunch of friends. When I arrived, Sheri was all aglow and kept placing my hand on her stomach until I felt the baby too. It was so cool to feel that little life stirring inside of her.

On Monday, September 23, something went wrong.

It was mid-afternoon, and I had just finished playing golf at Mt. Meadows Golf Course. When I stopped by the APU track office afterwards, Kevin told me that Sheri had called him and was very upset. I was supposed to call the hospital where she worked immediately. When I did, one of her coworkers told me to get over to Sheri's doctor's office right away.

A good friend of Sheri's, Senene Owen, stood in the waiting room, and from the look on her face I could tell something serious had happened. Sheri waited alone for me in one of the examining rooms. When I walked in, she clutched onto me and burst into tears.

"My baby's dead!" she blurted out in anguish.

"What do you mean?" I said, stunned. "Are you sure?"

"I listened for the heartbeat after lunch, but couldn't find it, so I had them scan me and I found out it had died!"

I just held her there as she sobbed, and I shed a few tears of my own. Not even twenty-four hours ago I'd felt the baby move, and I'd wondered what he or she would look like. Sheri and I had just spent a fun weekend fixing up things around the house and making a list of stuff we'd need for the nursery. And now—no baby. I was upset, but Sheri was devastated. She had so desperately wanted a child, and now it seemed that it had been taken away from her. I think I felt more grief for Sheri than for myself. We both knew this pregnancy was a miracle since it had taken us so long to get pregnant, but now that miracle was gone.

The doctor came back in and scanned Sheri with the ultrasound one last time. It was true.

After a moment Sheri sat up. "OK," she said firmly, "I want to get this baby out of me—right away." The doctor agreed to do the procedure at Sheri's hospital, where she felt more comfortable.

We drove home in silence, and Sheri picked up a few clothes. She guessed she'd be at the hospital for one or two nights at the most, and then it would all be over. At 6 p.m. we checked into the hospital. For the next day or two, Sheri would be a patient instead of a nurse.

When the lady at the admitting desk asked what the diagnosis was, Sheri replied, "Fetal demise"—the proper term, but it seemed so chilling.

I waited with her for the doctor in the Labor and Delivery wing. Since the NICU—the neonatal intensive care unit, where Sheri worked—was nearby, a group of her girlfriends came in and hung out in the room for a while. It seemed a little weird, since they all knew what was going on and yet were laughing and joking around, Sheri included. When the doctor walked in at around 9 p.m. and saw all the merriment, he got a strange look on his face.

"I know, I'm in denial," Sheri said to him. "But I realize I'm going to have to deal with this at some point."

The doctor gave her a drug to induce labor. Normally it would cause contractions to begin within a few hours, but for some reason it didn't work. Instead, she got violently sick, and I stayed up with her the entire night. By morning she seemed worse: she was weak, exhausted, and dehydrated, and she still hadn't gone into labor. I felt so helpless as I watched everyone changing the medication, giving her more fluids, and checking all her vital signs. They switched to a different labor-inducing drug, but it didn't work either. All day Tuesday and all night she just lay there in a semi-comatose state.

I was scared—so scared, in fact, that I never left the hospital. I stayed right there in her room, holding her hand, talking to her even though she rarely responded, and praying. She looked so terrible that I honestly thought she might die. Senene, Sheri's friend who was also an intensive care nurse, was so concerned that she stayed all night Tuesday to keep an eye on her. Sheri's mom and her sister, Sheli, had flown down. Pastor Roy Halberg, Jack, Kevin, Coach Franson, and all kinds of people stopped in.

Still no change. Finally, on Wednesday morning, nearly forty hours after Sheri had checked into the hospital, the doctor gave her an epidural, a spinal anesthesia that numbs you from the chest down. It would relieve the pain and make it possible for them to give her pitocin, a stronger drug for inducing labor.

Again, she slept all day, and there seemed to be little indication that this third method would work. In the meantime, I talked with Sheri's mom and sister and the other visitors and tried to catch a little sleep of my own.

Then around 8 p.m., she woke up screaming in pain, and I ran for the nurse. Strong contractions had kicked in very suddenly, and most of her anesthesia had worn off, so all sorts of people rushed in to administer more painkiller and assist with the delivery. It happened very quickly—a couple of pushes by Sheri and the baby was out. I couldn't believe my eyes: It was a tiny, tiny little boy, fully formed but no bigger than the palm of my hand. Nothing at all looked wrong with it. What could have caused it to die?

The nurse wrapped it in a little towel and let Sheri hold it for a minute as I watched. She thought it looked just like me. Then she handed it back to the nurse and immediately fell asleep.

What a bizarre and tragic experience. My emotions were so overloaded that I hardly knew what I was feeling. Mostly I was relieved that Sheri was OK. The doctor had examined her and given the approval for her to go home. At the hospital the next morning I was surprised and thankful to see her up and walking around. After barely moving from her bed in three days, she was taking a shower and even putting on some makeup.

As we were leaving, the woman who prepares birth certificates came around and asked if we'd like one for our baby. I hadn't even thought of it, but Sheri said yes.

"Well," the woman said, "have you thought of a name for the baby?"

Sheri and I looked at each other. Almost simultaneously we said, "How about Genesis?"

Genesis. Don't ask me why that name popped into both of our heads at once. It's certainly not a name I would normally choose for a child. But it seemed right for this one. Genesis stood for the beginning of something. Maybe our traumatic experience with this baby would signify some kind of beginning in our lives.

"Yes," Sheri said, "we'll name the baby Genesis."

I had wheeled her over to the NICU while we waited for the birth certificate to be processed. This time she and her friends were laughing over a wacky story in a copy of the *National Enquirer* someone had brought in. But when the woman returned with the birth certificate, Sheri took one look at the words "Genesis Johnson" and started bawling.

It had been a long and difficult week. It was time to go home.

That was September. There were still three months left in this incredibly trying year. In October, it was my turn to visit the hospital. I had decided to go ahead with exploratory surgery to identify and repair the problem with my knee. Dr. Shields of the Jobe Kerlin Group performed the surgery. All he could find was plica, a kind of fatty tissue. Removing it did not appear to take care of the problem, however, because once I was able to return to the track, it continued to hurt just like before. So the doctor tried a cortizone injection, which seemed to help a little.

As I struggled to get my knee back into shape, we both struggled with the loss of the baby—Sheri especially. She sank into a deep depression that would last for a number of months. I grieved over losing our child, but even more I hated to see Sheri hurting so much. At one point I wrote in my journal:

> I would give both of my knees to have our baby back. I would give anything. I'm confident we will have another chance. The Lord has blessed our marriage in many ways already. And I know he has a lot more to do with us. I feel him telling me to be patient and all will be OK in his time.

■ ■ ■

Between my injury and getting whipped by Dan, I worried a little during the fall that my major sponsors would lose interest in me. My world ranking had dropped to eight, and my U.S. ranking to two, behind Dan. Would they start to think of me as past my prime, a has-been?

A phone call from Tom Shepard of VISA after their October camp at Emory University made it clear the answer was no. They wanted to feature me and several other athletes in a network commercial highlighting their sponsorship of the '92 Olympic Games. Within a couple of weeks a film crew showed up and I did the spot in the L.A. Coliseum on my sore knee. I didn't run, but I was able to throw the javelin. They paid me very well for the day's work, but more importantly, the experience gave me a major confidence boost at a low time in my life.

Then came Reebok.

Chester Wheeler had invited Sheri and me to Orlando for Reebok's annual convention. Dan would be coming too, and it seemed they wanted to talk to us about something. He didn't say exactly what, but I figured it would be some kind of overview of the ways they wanted to use us in the coming year. Since Dan had done so well this year, I guessed they'd feature him as their main man and that I'd be more in the background. We hadn't done anything together for Reebok at this point. Maybe he'd do a commercial like the Pump spot I'd done earlier.

They put us up in one of the nice Disney hotels, and gave us free passes to Disney World, Sea World, and Universal Studios. Other than a few appearances at the convention, Sheri and I were able to relax and enjoy ourselves. But I kept wondering what this meeting would be about.

Finally, a day or two before the convention ended, David Ropes, Reebok's executive vice-president of advertising, and Chester brought Dan and Sheri and me together. They had something special they wanted to show us, something they needed our opinion on. They took us aside to a closet-sized room with a TV set, a VCR, and a few chairs. To one side was a stack of sneakers. *Oh,* I thought, *they've come up with a new shoe they want us to endorse. They're probably going to name a shoe The Decathlon, and then take a few pictures of Dan and me wearing it.*

David sat us down and said that Reebok and its advertising agency, Chiat/Day/Mojo, had come up with a few ideas for commercials we might be in, and asked us to watch a videotape.

What I saw on the screen made my mouth fall open.

It was a series of commercials—in the form of rough sketches—highlighting the rivalry between Dan and me for the '92 Olympic gold medal. Not just two or three commercials, but fifteen or twenty of them. "Dan does this. Dave does this. Who is the world's greatest athlete?" Over and over, the same basic idea with a different twist each time, all ending with the words, "To be settled in Barcelona."

This was big. *Man, if they do this,* I thought, *they're going to be spending gobs of money. We'll be their main advertising campaign.*

"So what do you think?" David said as he flipped on the lights. "We want to feature you guys in these commercials. Are you interested?"

Dan and I looked at each other, wide-eyed. Was this really happening? I needed to pinch myself to make sure I wasn't dreaming. And Sheri looked as if she was about to say, "Is this some kind of joke? Are we on Candid Camera?"

"Well," I said with a grin, "let me think about it." I paused for one second. "Yes." Dan did the same thing.

Then David said they wanted to run four fifteen-second spots right during the upcoming Super Bowl, the event watched by more people than anything else on TV. At that time a thirty-second spot cost $850,000, so the package would add up to more than a million and a half. We'd need to film the commercials within the next couple of weeks.

I was amazed that they were really going to invest all this money in Dan and me—$25 million in all. It would certainly give the decathlon more visibility in this country than ever before. But even more, I marveled that God was providing this as a vehicle for me to represent him before the world. It would open up many doors for me to talk about my Christian faith. I thought back to when I first started doing the decathlon, sitting there blasting music in my car at Linn-Benton. All during that time I'd had the feeling that great things were going to happen in my life through this sport, and that God had brought it into my life for a reason. Now, here it was, an opportunity that had exceeded my wildest dreams. And it had even happened after a bad year.

That night, they played the same videotape for the entire convention of Reebok employees, distributors, and retail operators to let them in on their upcoming advertising plans. Then they called us up to say a few words. Dan was gracious, and said that he was honored to be a part of the campaign. But for some reason I wanted to have fun and play up the rivalry, so I read a silly poem I'd quickly written about who the world's greatest athlete was, making no bones about the fact that it was Dave.

As I sat down, I felt pretty good. But I also felt the soreness in my knee and thought, *Dang, I sure hope my knee gets better so I can make the team.*

Dan and I had fun shooting the commercials. It helped us get to know each other better. But let me tell you—it took a lot of work. We completed eleven commercials in ten days, going from sunup to sundown at the Los Angeles Coliseum and Mt. SAC. I was completely exhausted at the end of most days. I couldn't believe all the different people involved—makeup artists, hair stylists, camera and sound crews, producers, directors, representatives from Reebok and from Chiat/Day/Mojo, even caterers. All of them seemed overworked, and by the time we had finished, I could tell why. It still amazed me that after twelve hours of shooting, they'd use fifteen, or at most, thirty seconds of footage for the final product. Dan and I turned the shoots into acting competitions, each trying to finish our part in fewer takes. And of course, each of us thought we were the better actor.

There were a few especially memorable moments during the filming, such as the time Dan and I had to scream at each other with our faces six inches apart for the "who makes the most noise" spot. My voice was completely gone after that one.

And it was extra special having Sheri, my mom, Coach Franson, Pastor Roy Halberg, and Ade Olokaju (as my "mailman") serve as the "objective" Americans who picked me to win the gold. All of Dan's supporters for that clip were real, too—except his ex-girlfriend!

Super Bowl Sunday finally arrived—January 26, 1992—and Sheri and I invited a whole bunch of friends over for a Super Bowl party—or was it a Dan and Dave party? The first spot had baby pictures of Dan and me. The second had photos of us at age four, and the third at age seven. The fourth showed us both competing for the first time. Each time there was the question, "Who is the world's greatest athlete?" Everyone in the house went wild. When I called my parents, they were crying for joy because their little boy was on TV. I began to sense a platform being built for me to talk about the Lord.

Every few weeks a new commercial debuted. Newspapers, magazines, and TV shows—not to mention millions of viewers—began wondering who Dan and Dave were. People started recognizing me when I went places. On the track I signed hundreds of autographs, and at Pacific Sports, Mike and Bob were getting more calls than they could handle for speaking and possible sponsorships.

It truly amazed me to see myself so often on the tube. Suddenly, all the things I had dreamed the decathlon would do had happened—except, of course, winning the gold medal, which lay ahead. I had become one of the most well-known athletes in the country.

My friends and "family" at Azusa Pacific University played a key role throughout the whole experience by not letting my head get too big. Most of the people there continued to treat me just like they always had—like one of the family. They kept me humble. Not that they weren't happy for me—they were very excited both for me and for the opportunity I would have to tell my story. And I think they knew that they were an important part of that story. But they reminded me that no matter how great an athlete I would become, or how short of my goals I would fall, the Lord would love me just the same.

He didn't require perfection; he didn't even require me to be the best in the world. All he asked is that I give one hundred percent for him. As far as Jesus was concerned, I wasn't Dave the hot-shot decathlete, or Dave the famous guy on TV. To him, I was just Dave, his servant, his warrior, his child.

What kept me steady amid all the distractions and temptations was my faith that the road God had set before me was the right one, and that he would give me the strength to stay on that road and reach the goals that it would lead me to. All the other things—the big sponsorships, the public recognition, the TV commercials, the money—were important, but secondary to my true purpose, which was to follow the road Christ had laid out for me. I could use the "extras" as motivators to help me achieve my goals, but only if I kept them in proper perspective and remembered that they were on the *side* of the road—they weren't the road itself. Otherwise they'd distract me or lure me off the road altogether. Appearing in all those commercials, for instance, gave me extra motivation to train hard, not so I could be more famous or make more money, but so I could be the very best for the Lord and have more opportunities to talk about him.

Because of my sore knee, I'd hardly trained at all in January and February. But the third cortizone injection by the doctor "took" and I suddenly was pain-free. For the next six weeks, I worked out long and hard, spurred by the extra pressure of those commercials and bolstered by another great VISA camp in New Orleans, the site of the upcoming Olympic Trials. I got myself in such great shape that in my first meet of the year, the Mt. SAC Relays at Azusa, I actually came within striking distance of the world record. I PR'd in four events and racked up 8727 points, my all-time best. I felt good and extremely focused for the entire meet, and it showed. The score gave me the big boost I needed to carry me into the Trials.

The publicity and the pressure grew in the weeks that followed. Everywhere I went, it seemed, people noticed "that Dave guy" or "that Dan-and-Dave guy." We appeared on magazine covers and talk shows. People stopped me constantly for autographs and pictures. In offices around the country, people were placing bets on Dan or Dave. I wasn't used to this kind of attention, but I tried to stay focused and concentrated on my training.

About two weeks before the Trials, I was working out with Kevin, running a 350 sprint for time. As I rounded the final corner, I felt a pop in my right foot—the same one I'd injured back in 1987. I clocked one of my fastest times, but I could tell something major was wrong. The foot had been bothering me some recently, but nothing like this. The pop was painful, but also seemed to release some pressure. I called Coach Franson, who was at a conference, and told him what had happened. It felt like a bone spur again.

Oh, great.

As before, the x-ray proved inconclusive, and the doctor agreed that the bone spur had probably grown back. I took it easy the rest of the week, but I still wanted to compete at the Trials. I found that if I bound the foot with a special arch support wrap, it seemed to relieve the pain.

Coach, Kevin, and I arrived in New Orleans early for the Trials and tried to get in some light training. One day my foot would hurt, and the next it would feel great, so we decided to keep it tightly wrapped and hope for the best.

With all the media frenzy over the Trials, and especially over the Dan and Dave rivalry, I hardly had time to worry about my foot. I would have distracted myself by exploring the city with Kevin, except that all the reporters and others who recognized me made it nearly impossible to go out. So instead, we did a lot of hanging out in my hotel room.

Mike Bone of Pacific Sports, working with Azusa Pacific University's public relations director, Guy Adams, had made some creative hotel arrangements. They had found out that there were two big hotels across the street from each other— one of which was putting up Dan and his coaches. So they approached the other hotel and talked them into giving us a series of free rooms. In return, Mike (through Reebok) inundated the hotel staff with Dave shirts and hats, and I agreed to speak to them after the competition. Mike joked that they had transformed the place into the Hotel Dave.

I couldn't believe the room Kevin and I had. It was the Presidential Suite, and it looked like a huge luxury condominium, with two bedrooms and two baths. Kevin stayed in one room and I had the other. Sheri, her mom, and Sheri's friend Senene, who were sharing the room next door, came in and goofed off with us. Between watching TV coverage of the other track and field events of the Trials, playing Mario Bros. on our Gameboys, and ordering pizzas, we managed to occupy ourselves. I did interviews with NBC, the VISA people, and one or two others.

Finally the big day arrived, and Coach Franson, Kevin, and I headed over to Tad Gormley Stadium. It was hot and humid outside—over 90 degrees—and slightly windy. In spite of the sore ankle, I felt ready. I'd been through two previous Olympic Trials, and knew that my primary task was to relax and earn a spot on the team.

I wasn't prepared for what I saw when we got there. Reebok was handing out thousands of hats, t-shirts, fans, buttons, even pencils and pens—red ones with Dan's name, and blue ones with mine. The crowd, which numbered only a few thousand at first, swelled to more than 17,000 by the end of the day. They were all going wild over the Dan and Dave competition.

Dan and I said a brotherly hello to each other before running out on the field. When our names were called, the crowd roared.

I had an average but consistent first day, with a PR in the shot put and a near-PR in the 400. During that race, the last of the day, I was in my final turn when a huge moth flew into my mouth. It startled me, but after six or seven strides I managed to spit it out and still finished strong. Fortunately, I had not sucked it in while taking a deep breath. After five events I was in fifth place, with my best day ahead of me. My sore ankle had held up fine. If I didn't make any mistakes tomorrow, I'd earn my ticket to Barcelona.

Dan had an incredible first day, setting a new world record with his score of 4698. It looked like another showdown between us for the top two spots. But again, I was concentrating more on making the team than beating Dan.

On Day Two, I opened with a shaky hurdle race, trying to be cautious of my foot. Then I threw a solid discus. After seven events, I had moved up to second place behind Dan, who still commanded a 500-point lead.

Then the unexpected happened.

We were preparing to pole vault. Warmups went well for everyone, including Dan and me. We were both clearing sixteen feet easily. I decided to open at 15'9", a height that I knew would not cause much stress. Dan chose the same. I was nervous, but having been in that situation before, I cleared on my first attempt.

Dan's situation was slightly more precarious. He'd been injured early in the season and had not vaulted in a meet all spring—though he'd practiced a lot. His PR was over seventeen feet, so no one, including me, ever thought he'd have a problem. Apparently, he was feeling pretty nervous, however. And he'd never been in a situation quite like this before—the pressure of being in the Olympic Trials, with millions watching on TV and millions of your sponsor's dollars riding on your performance. The sweltering heat and humidity didn't help either.

When he missed on his first attempt, I was concerned. I saw the lack of confidence in his face. But I still thought he'd recover.

On the second try, he gained enough height, but landed on the bar and knocked it off.

Now I worried. If he didn't clear on this attempt, he'd get zero points for the event and lose his chance to go to Barcelona. Sitting in the shade with a wet towel around my neck, I told myself that it was not the Lord's plan for Dan to miss this height and miss the Games. I felt sure that Dan would make it this time.

But the pressure had become too great. On his last try, he started and stopped twice before committing himself. When he finally approached the bar, I thought he had good speed. But as soon as he planted the pole, I noticed a major hesitation. He knew he wasn't going to make it. The fear had become greater than the athlete, and it had blocked his focus beyond recovery. No athletic ability in the world can survive such a foreign and debilitating feeling. If he had experienced this situation before, his mind and muscle memory would have adjusted and he would have cleared the bar.

But today, before a hushed crowd, he didn't.

I lost control and swore out loud, only to be captured by a TV camera and broadcast to the world. (I lamely told a reporter afterwards that I'd said "Oh shoot," but the truth was embarrassingly obvious.) So many emotions were racing through my mind. First, I was angry at Dan for altering the Dan and Dave plan. What would Reebok do now? What about all the money they were spending, the commercials they still hadn't aired, the publicity and sales they were counting on? I was also mad at an Olympic qualifying system that would prevent one of the world's best athletes from going to the games because of one mistake.

My second thought was *Wow—it's going to be just my show now. I don't have to worry about Dan beating me. I'm going to win the Trials and the Olympic Games for sure, or at least it'll be a lot easier.*

But then, as I saw him drop to the pit in anguish, I put myself in his place. In 1985, I had no-heighted twice in less important but still national-level meets. It's the worst feeling in the world, and it happens to nearly all decathletes at some point. But to have it happen at the Olympic Trials must be devastating. Dan had trained so hard the past few years, and he'd overcome many obstacles to become the reigning world champion. I knew how badly he wanted to make this Olympic team. From the very start, I had wanted us both to be in Barcelona. Now a big part of me would be missing there. I had been training to beat Dan at the Games. He'd been training to beat me. There was no one better than he or I in the world.

He was walking around the vaulting area in agony and disbelief. He seemed lost and unsure of what to do with himself. I got up and made my way over to him. When we made eye contact, he turned away, but I knew he was hurting. With tears in my eyes, I put my arms around him and simply said, "I am so sorry, Dan." I truly cared for him and how he must have been feeling. At that moment, I cared very little about myself. No other words were spoken.

Then I tried to collect myself for the rest of my own vaulting. I did well, clearing over seventeen feet, but I was still distracted over Dan's misfortune. Many of the red Dan hats and wind fans in the crowd were being replaced by blue Dave ones, and I felt the pressure of the whole Reebok campaign shifting over to me. Thankfully, I was able to hold on to my goals and my deeper purpose during the final two events. I set a new American record in the javelin and then ran an average 1500 to win the meet with 8649 points. Just as Dan's first-day score had broken the world record, so had my second-day total of 4455.

The headlines the next day said, "It's Dave!" I was thrilled to make the team, but it wasn't supposed to turn out this way. Even though Dan belonged there, he wouldn't be at the Games. Meets in the United States and even world meets paled next to the aura and the challenge of the Olympics. For a decathlete truly to earn the title of "world's greatest athlete," he must win the Olympic gold medal, and Dan wouldn't have that chance.

Reebok recovered well from the incident, though not without a whirlwind of frantic meetings and phone calls and press conferences. They reaffirmed their commitment to both Dan and me, and in a very classy move, they decided to shoot several new commercials with Dan supporting my road to Barcelona. It was typical of the family approach they had toward their athletes and employees.

Amidst all the chaos, Chester made time to take the entire "Dave contingent" out to eat at a very fancy restaurant in New Orleans. He said that while we all felt sad for Dan, we should not let it detract from my victory and my second-day world record.

As I thought about going to the Games without Dan, I tried to accept that God must have had something different in mind for him.

I would soon discover the same was true for me.

Javelin

PR: 244'8"

I love to throw things. I always have. Maybe that's why I've excelled in the javelin more than any other event. It's my best and also my favorite. I look forward to the javelin because I know I'm going to make a big move on the field pointwise at this point in the decathlon. If I'm in the lead when it comes to the javelin, there's no hope for anybody. I'm going to win. Guaranteed.

The javelin is the third and last of the throws. For once, you're not restricted to a throwing circle: you can take as long and as fast a runup to the throwing line as you want, which allows you to give the javelin a lot more velocity. That's the way I like to throw. I want to be free, and I want that javelin to soar.

Because it comes so naturally, I think I understand the javelin better than most other decathletes. It's not just an implement that I use to get points. Somehow it has become part of me, an extension of myself. It's a thing of beauty that wants to live, and it is my job to give it life.

I love to watch the javelin float, and to hear the "Ooooo" of the crowd as they follow its flight. The longer it stays up there, the more the sound of the crowd builds. None of the other events has that sense of awe and beauty.

If I were a javelin, I'd want to be thrown by someone who understood me and who would do justice to who I was. For that kind of person I would want to fly very, very far. I'd want to experience that feeling of floating, of looking down on the crowd as they gazed and gasped. I honestly think I'm doing a disservice to the javelin if I don't give it enough velocity that it can really fly. When I send it off with a nice long scream, I want it to scream back at me from the air, "Thanks, Dave—thanks for giving me life!"

My favorite experience with the javelin took place at a VISA camp after the Barcelona Games. I'd recently had ankle surgery, and I wasn't planning on participating in any of the events because my foot hadn't fully healed yet. But as I sat there in my jeans watching the javelin practice, I thought I'd give it a try just for fun. People were throwing around 180 feet, and I figured I could make that distance even though my foot was still sore.

We were allowed to choose a piece of music to accompany our throw. Most of the others were playing head-banger rock tunes to get themselves fired up. But when my turn came and I stood alone out in the field, the music I had arranged to come over the speakers was the Joe Cocker song "You Are So Beautiful." It's a mellow, moving, romantic song, one that I knew the javelin would appreciate. I saw it as a tribute to the javelin itself. Upon hearing the music, everyone immediately burst into laughter.

I didn't care. I took a short approach and let her fly.

The laughter stopped as we all watched that javelin soar. It floated in the air for quite a while before it landed 225 feet away.

"You stink!" everyone joked in amazement. "How can you stroll out here in your jeans and make a throw like that?"

I couldn't believe it myself. But maybe it had something to do with my appreciation of the javelin's beauty.

To me, the javelin speaks of the need to enjoy things of beauty in our life and work. Beauty is all around us, but we often allow it to go unnoticed. The javelin also reminds me that we all have things we're really good at, and that we should appreciate them and thank God for giving us those gifts. Even people who feel they can't do anything well have some kind of special gift from God. They might have to look a little harder to see it, but it is there nonetheless, waiting to be used and appreciated.

■ ■ ■

chapter ten

THE PAIN IN SPAIN

BESIDES DAN'S elimination from the Olympic team, one other thing cast a shadow over my victory at the Trials: My ankle felt worse afterwards. When I got home and tried to train on it, the pain and swelling grew so intense that I had to stop running altogether.

I wasn't satisfied with the doctor's diagnosis of a bone spur, so Coach Franson and I went to see another podiatrist, Dr. Landry. He took a special kind of x-ray known as an MRI bone scan, which picks up things that ordinary x-rays cannot. Sure enough, he discovered that my problem was not a bone spur, but a stress fracture to the navicular bone. Furthermore, the scan showed that the bone had been previously broken in the same place.

It was then that it suddenly hit me: the bone spur I *thought* I had in 1987 when I stepped on the shot had actually been a stress fracture. No wonder it had given me so much pain back then. A few weeks ago when I felt my foot pop, I must have *re*broken the same bone. Then I had pounded on it for the Trials.

So much for the explanation. Now I had to face the present reality: very little could be done about it.

I'm not sure who was more upset—Coach or me. When he first told me, there was such despair in his face that I said, "Coach, you look terrible. C'mon, you've gotta help me out here."

"Yeah, I know," he sighed, "I'm just trying to deal with it right now."

I wanted to scream and cry. It wasn't fair. Only three weeks before the start of the Olympic Games, and I was favored to win the gold medal.

Franson had a long discussion with the doctors, and then we all sat down together. With lots of taping and a battery of special machines that would reduce some of the pain, it might still be possible for me to compete. Painful, but possible.

How would I deal with all that pain? When it strikes in an area like your foot, it affects your whole performance. You don't step on it the same, you don't push off from it the same, and there's nothing you can do about it—your brain simply shuts it down. But even more than the physical pain, I wondered how I'd handle the emotional pain of not reaching my ultimate goals. With those two strikes against me, it would be the greatest challenge of my life just to survive all ten events. Would it be worth it?

Coach and I both knew that we'd come too far to stop now. There had to be some kind of reason for this. I was scared to death, but I decided to go for it.

There was no way I'd be able to get through this ordeal alone; no one knew that better than me. So Coach Franson sat down and tried to create a master plan that would keep me in the best possible condition—physical, mental, and spiritual— to compete with a fractured foot. He knew he needed to head off all the factors that would discourage me and cripple my mental and spiritual readiness.

He couldn't do a whole lot with the physical part. I underwent all kinds of therapy with the doctors and the various machines. I worked out a few times in the swimming pool to maintain my fitness level without putting weight on my foot. I also rode the stationary bike and did some low-impact cross-training exercises. It was nowhere near the kind of training I needed to be doing to get myself mentally ready, but it was something. Fortunately, my training throughout the season had been strong and I was in good overall shape.

He also spent many hours with the doctors, going over all the possible "what if" scenarios from a medical standpoint and working out contingency plans. The various foot therapy machines would accompany me to Barcelona, and U.S. Olympic Committee doctors would be available at all times to treat the foot if it was injured further. They didn't want to give me injections for the pain unless I absolutely needed them, however, because the numbness might render the foot unusable.

To keep me from getting too mentally uptight, Coach even backed off from some of his own contact with me. He was always available if I needed him, but he also knew that since he was Coach, his very presence would at times make me nervous about the Games. So he enlisted Kevin as kind of a buffer to hang out with me and keep me calm and positive. He'd stay with me during my therapy and the occasional workouts, and room with me at the Games. That way Franson would be free to handle all the behind-the-scenes details and arrangements and medical considerations without involving me.

Early on we decided to keep the whole situation a secret. If I was to do well at the Games—or even finish, for that matter—I would have to maintain the most positive attitude I could muster. I needed to think about my foot as little as possible. So we agreed to tell no more than a handful of our closest friends, so they could pray for us, and, of course, the necessary medical people. Coach would have to inform the USOC doctors. I didn't even tell my parents or Sheri the full extent of the problem: I only said that my foot was sore and that I had a bone spur.

We felt it was too risky to tell Reebok or VISA about the injury. Reebok had a $25 million campaign riding on Dan and Dave, but with Dan out of the Olympic picture, the last thing they needed to hear was that Dave had a broken foot. And since we honestly didn't know what the outcome would be, we figured that involving them would put even more pressure on my shoulders. Even worse, the news might be leaked to the press. If the media were to get wind of my injury, they'd be hounding me day and night with questions about my foot, which would cause me to focus on it too much. Plus, the other countries and decathletes would then find out and have a mental advantage. I knew I wouldn't be able to handle the negative feelings all the publicity would stir up. So when people asked me how training was going, I'd just smile and say, "I'm ready to go after the gold medal."

On the inside, of course, my stomach was in knots. It was the strangest time of my life, with so many conflicting emotions. I felt tossed between what I wanted from the world—victory and glory—and what the Lord needed from me. Without a great wife and supportive friends, I would never have made it through that difficult time.

I stayed in the States a week longer than the other Olympic athletes. When I left to meet Kevin in Europe in mid-July, I had only done one running workout since the Trials, even though I should have been doing two or three running workouts a week, running really fast to build my confidence. We spent a week in southern France to avoid the media and do some very light training. Coach Franson joined us toward the end of that time.

So far, Coach's master plan seemed to be working. I arrived at the Games feeling afraid, but ready to do my best. Kevin and Coach were even telling me I could win the whole thing. Mentally, I knew I could win. I knew I could even break the world record. The main question was whether my foot would hold up. Coach introduced me to the four USOC doctors who knew all about my condition and would be providing medical care throughout the decathlon. I had stayed in the athletes' village for one night, but feared a repeat of the noise and distraction in Seoul, so the three of us stayed at a hotel in Barcelona instead. It turned out that Reebok had reserved a bank of rooms in the same hotel. They were all excited about the decathlon and couldn't wait to see the outcome. I'm sure they would have had instant coronaries if they'd known I was injured.

Before the competition Reebok and VISA sponsored a big gathering of decathletes and invited the past U.S. gold medalists—Bruce Jenner, Bill Toomey, Rafer Johnson, Milt Campbell, and Bob Mathias. As I sat there listening to them, I felt sad that I most likely would never join their ranks. But another part of me still believed a miracle might happen and I could win the Games.

We also had to attend a big press conference with mostly American media. For an hour and a half, Coach and I would have to answer all their questions about how I'd approach the Games, how it felt to not have Dan there, who my main competition would be, and so on. We were worried that if the news about my injury had somehow been leaked, it might come out at this press conference. Just in case, Coach had talked to the USOC doctors about how to handle the situation. They said that if any medical questions came up, we could refer them to the USOC to answer. They had prepared a brief statement that would give a little information and then close the issue, something like, "Dave has a problem with his foot, but we have determined that he can compete on it, and right now our focus is on that gold medal performance."

Fortunately, the press conference went fine, and the issue didn't come up. But one sportswriter from the *Los Angeles Times,* Randy Harvey, suspected the injury. Although I didn't know it, he'd been calling all kinds of people in the States, and had found out that I was getting some special treatment on my foot. After the press conference, he started walking in our direction. Coach Franson, knowing that this reporter was on the trail, headed him off before he reached me.

"You're Randy Harvey," Coach said. "You've sure been doing a lot of homework."

"Yes I have," he said. "What's up?"

"Well, there is a problem," Franson said, "but before I go any further, I need to say that we've had a plan for dealing with the problem, and we need you to respect our wishes about exposing the information."

"What are you asking me to do?"

"Not to print until we give the go-ahead, and then we'll give you first shot at the story. It's very important to us." He went on to explain briefly that it could seriously hurt my chances for the gold medal if the word got out.

After thinking for a minute, Harvey said, "OK, I can do that."

So Franson said, "You're right, there's a problem with Dave's foot. I'll give you all the details on the second day of the decathlon. I'll let you know where I'll be sitting, so you can talk to me and have the story before anybody else." I was pretty impressed by the way Coach handled that reporter, who, by the way, was true to his word.

Other than appearing for a few TV interviews, including one with Bruce Jenner, I sequestered myself in the hotel with Kevin as much as possible and kept up the foot therapy. I felt weird during the interview with Bruce; he kept trying to get me to predict a score, and I simply couldn't, given my condition.

Meanwhile, Sheri, her parents, and my parents had arrived. I later learned that there had been a mixup about their hotel arrangements, but they had managed to work things out. Our parents stayed on a Cunard cruise ship sponsored by Kodak. And Bruce and his wife, Kris, graciously offered Sheri an extra hotel room they weren't using. Other welcome guests were Azusa Pacific University president Richard Felix, his wife, Vivian, and Guy Adams, the school's public relations director, and his wife, Shelly. Guy was a tremendous help with transportation, food, lodging and other needs throughout the Trials and our time in Barcelona.

I woke up on the morning of the first day of competition and gingerly stepped out of bed. I knew the pounding my foot was about to take, and I was scared. I was afraid of injuring it worse so that I would never run again. Afraid of failing in front of so many people. Afraid of disappointing all the friends and relatives who were part of my Olympic dream. I had wanted to be an inspiration to them, and instead, I felt I was going to let them down.

Coach Franson, Kevin, and I had breakfast at the hotel. Like me, they were afraid for my foot, sad over the possibility of losing, and mostly disappointed that I had to go to the

Games like this. But they also felt a sense of anticipation, a sense that something special was happening. They were confident that I'd do my best, and believed that my best, even under such tough conditions, just might be enough to win.

We checked in at the beautiful Olympic Stadium at 7 a.m., and I loosened up a little on the warmup track outside the facility. My foot had been heavily taped. *Make sure these guys don't see you limping,* I said to myself, trying to walk normally. I felt some pain, but not too much. I also sensed that people were looking at me, since I was favored to win. If they only knew.

The stadium was mostly empty at 9 when we lined up for the 100 meters. Two false starts, and finally we took off. It felt great to let my body give one hundred percent again. Halfway through the race, however, I felt a stabbing pain in my foot, so sharp I slowed up a bit to relieve it. My time of 11.16 was only average, and I needed above-average scores if I was to win. But I reminded myself that this was the decathlon, and anything could happen. Looking up at the replay of the race on the stadium monitors, I could tell I was already favoring my right leg; fortunately, no one else seemed to notice. Then a weird thing happened: Dan's face suddenly flashed on the monitor for about three seconds. No sound, no identification, just his face. NBC had brought him in to help with some of their Triplecast commentary.

Coach Franson and Kevin stopped down to offer a few words of encouragement before I began the long jump. I warmed up some, but not as much as I would have liked. On my first attempt I stepped over the toeboard for a foul, but made surprisingly good distance. My second jump was just over 24 feet, good considering the speed I was losing on the approach. On the third I fouled again.

The knife in my foot during the 100 had given me a scare. During the shot put I received an even greater scare, one unrelated to the injury. I told myself that this event should be reasonably stress-free, requiring no fancy footwork. I'd have to push off with my sore foot, but the pain would be brief. On my first throw, it hurt as I began, hurt when I uncoiled and released, then hurt again as I stopped myself. But not too bad. The official called a foul, however. Then, on my second throw, the red flag went up again. Neither one felt like a foul to me.

Now things were getting serious. *Relax, it's OK,* I said to myself, *you still have another throw. No one fouls three throws.* A third foul would mean zero points, and I'd be out of contention.

When my final turn came, I threw a little more cautiously just to make sure I was legal. But when I looked over at the mustachioed official, he was holding up the red flag yet again.

No way!

I couldn't believe it. I'd just been called for my third foul. I was out. Pack up and go home. But I just knew I hadn't stepped on top of the toeboard; I knew I'd made a legal throw. I went back into the ring and stood there, demanding an explanation.

"Hey, come and show me how I fouled," I said. "Show me what you saw."

No answer from the official—only a confused look.

"Do you speak English? Please show me what you saw."

The guy just stood there, not knowing what to do. And I refused to budge until somebody would talk to me. On the inside, I was nearly panicking. *There is no way I'm going to get this to go in my favor. Officials don't make mistakes at the Games. They're always right here—or at least they act like it. What am I going to do? It's over. This is hopeless. It can't end this way. I guess I should give up.*

Who knows what kind of suicidal thoughts were going through the heads of the Reebok people. Dan had blown the Trials. Now I had just blown the Games.

Then the head official came over and conferred with the flag man in Spanish. A couple of others joined the discussion. I paced back and forth near the ring, trying to figure out what was going on. Then I saw my throw being replayed three or four times on the big screen while the officials watched. Maybe I still had a chance.

Finally, the ruling came through from the head official: I had not fouled after all. And since no measurement had been taken of my third throw, I'd be given an unprecedented fourth attempt. It was a miracle.

Of course, I still needed to make a legal throw. As I picked up the shot and stepped back into the ring, however, the partisan Spanish crowd booed and whistled loudly in disapproval. What a drag—it wasn't my fault. I wondered if I should just take a standing throw to be safe. It would be too devastating to foul again. But then I knew I couldn't do that. God had provided this opportunity for a reason. He had never told me to give half an effort; he had always said to give one hundred percent.

Lord, help me with this, I prayed, trying to stop shaking. *I've never had to compete with the crowd against me before. Give me your strength, and help me to relax.*

I relaxed. I got myself set. Then I unleashed the biggest throw of my life—50'1¾". A PR by nearly a foot. *YEAH!*

The shot heard round the world.

The booing grew louder as I left the stadium, but I didn't care. Coach and Kevin were waiting for me, breathless over what had just happened. Sheri gave me a big kiss. Bruce Jenner congratulated me and said, "Boy, were you lucky." Yeah, maybe, but I think it was more than luck. It was the Lord announcing to the world that a story was beginning to unfold.

It was around 2 p.m., and the siesta break had begun. Since the high jump would not start until 5:30, we returned to the hotel. It was nice to get away from the track and relax a little. I knew it would not be easy to finish on my ankle, which was beginning to swell. I was well off the pace for a world record, but still believed I had a good chance for the gold. I had to trust that the Lord was in control.

Back at the stadium, I had difficulty warming up for the high jump. My legs were tired—the right one from the injury, and the left one from working harder to compensate. As a result, both my speed and my steps were off. When the event began, I needed to take extra jumps to clear heights I'd normally make on my first attempt. My frustration grew. Ironically, one thing that kept me from quitting was the unruly crowd, which continued to boo me every time my turn came. The anger they stirred up drove me to try harder. When the jumping finally ended nearly four hours later, I had only managed 6'6¾"—OK, but well short of what I needed.

I hung out with Coach and Kevin underneath the stadium, trying to distract myself while waiting for the 400 meters to start. The gold medal was slipping away. Nursing my sore ankle, I thought about home and my friends at Azusa Pacific and tried to put myself there in that positive, supportive environment. Coach and Kevin continued to encourage, helping me to get psyched up.

Under stadium lights and a near-capacity crowd, we lined up for the first heat of the 400 at about 9:30 p.m. I remembered something Bruce Jenner had told me at one of the VISA camps. He said that in 1976, he had let out all the stops and ran as hard as he could in the 400, figuring that he could rely upon the excitement of the Games to finish strong. So when the gun went off, I gave every ounce I had, with no attempt to conserve. I ran well until the last 100 meters, when the ankle pain and leg fatigue took over. I finished a full second slower than my average.

For the most part, I'd been able to mask the pain of my injury that first day. I probably looked normal to the announcers, TV viewers, even the other athletes. But after the 400, people began to wonder why I wasn't in peak form. Reporters came up to me and asked what was wrong, and so did some of the Reebok people. I brushed them off at first, saying I'd have the same kind of second day that I had at the Trials. But then I realized I needed to be more honest.

"Yes, there is something going on," I finally told them, without going into any detail. "I need to evaluate it overnight, and I'll let you know tomorrow after the hurdles."

I was in ninth place after five events, about 280 points out of first. I had trailed Dan by more than that on two previous occasions and still come back to win—but that was on a healthy foot. Coach was saying that it looked like this wouldn't be a high-scoring meet, perhaps only around 8600. I'd reached or surpassed that mark four times. No, I wouldn't break the world record as I'd hoped, but Coach and Kevin believed I still could grab the gold. It would take a miracle, but it was certainly possible. God had already provided one miracle during the shot put. He could perform another if he wanted to. He could take away the pain and allow me to have a tremendous second-day performance.

Back in my hotel room, I wasn't so sure. My battered, swollen foot hurt more than ever, and the machines didn't seem to help. The pain, combined with anticipation and anxiety over the next day's events, made it hard for me to sleep. As I lay there in bed, I became angry that God was allowing this happen to me. Why would he not want a gold medal to shine in my life for him? The Olympic Games was the perfect place for me to make an impact for Christ, especially after the visibility Reebok had provided. Tears welled up as I realized I had been preparing myself for tomorrow for ten years, only to have it taken away from me.

The Lord must have heard my anger and my questioning, because I began to feel a little reassured. He had not left me out in the cold. He was right there with me, still loving and caring for me, still working in my life. As much as I wanted that gold medal, maybe he was trying to tell me that something else was even more important. I remembered the goal he had first helped me to set—to take on the decathlon and life in general as Christ would. That goal hadn't changed—medal or no medal. In spite of the pain, in spite of the disappointment, I could aim for that goal with complete confidence. I was certainly not prepared physically for the challenge tomorrow would bring, but I could rely upon my spiritual preparation. I would have to move forward by faith.

I woke up very stiff the next morning, stiffer than usual because my whole body—especially my left leg—had been working overtime to compensate for my right ankle. For one second I wondered if the miracle I'd been hoping for had occurred, but my thoughts were rudely interrupted by the throbbing of my foot. I carefully got out of bed and reached for the ibuprofen.

As I warmed up for the hurdles, I tried to figure out what to tell the reporters; I had said their questions would be answered after this event. If anything would completely break my foot, it would be the hurdles. I would have to kick and come down ten times on that fractured bone with all my weight. On the other hand, Coach had been figuring that if I survived the hurdles, I'd most likely be able to finish the meet.

I barely survived. After the third or fourth hurdle, my foot popped again, and I nearly screamed in pain as I hung on for a 14.76 finish. X-rays after the games would show that the stress fracture had split further. *OK, more pain,* I thought as I sat down. *That's just great. Now what's going to happen?* Franson came down to see how I felt. I wanted to say, "Hey, I can't keep going, this is ridiculous."

"Look," he said, "the next event's the discus. It's not going to hurt to throw the discus."

With an ice pack on my ankle, I talked to the reporters who had clustered around me. I was competing on a stress fracture to the right foot, I explained. The injury had occurred two weeks before the Trials. I didn't have time to say much more than that, as we were being called over to start the discus. I figured I'd throw the discus and then call it a meet.

Amid continued boos from the crowd, I had a fine throw of more than 161 feet. A good note to end on. But then I wondered: *Was the Lord trying to tell me I was strong enough to keep going?*

My foot already felt worse than yesterday. To continue would risk injuring it still further. And if the physical pain wasn't bad enough, the emotional pain of not reaching my goals had begun to set in. I would not break the world record; I would not win the gold medal; and the way my foot was feeling, I wouldn't win any medal at all. What reason did I have to finish?

I talked it over with Coach and Kevin during the siesta break. I was trying to get them to say, "Well OK, don't finish," but they never would. Instead, their response was, "Why not just give it a try and see what happens?"

The prospect of pole vaulting frightened me even more than the hurdles. I worried that my injury would prevent me from gaining sufficient speed. If I ran too slow, the pole could whip me in the wrong direction and cause me to miss the pit completely. I cleared a couple of heights during warmups, but by the time the official vaulting began, my ankle was so swollen I could hardly tie my shoe. And the pain was excruciating, almost impossible to block out. With each attempt, I had to actively put the pain somewhere else and distract myself. Talking to God and asking for his protection helped.

At one point while I prepared to make my approach, the image of Jesus Christ carrying his cross came to mind. He had endured unimaginable pain in his journey, but had never given up. Suddenly the vaulting pole became my cross to bear, and because of what Christ had done for me, I wouldn't give up either. That picture inspired me to reach all the way to 16'8¾", even though my my foot was hurting worse by the minute.

When the bar went up to 17'¾" I had to switch to a bigger pole, one that requires you to run harder and faster. After two limping attempts, the pain simply became unbearable and I lost it. Angrily I threw down the pole, flung my chalk bag, and stormed off the field, leaving my poles behind. I was through.

Coach Franson and Kevin met me in the training room under the stadium. Utterly broken, I dropped into a chair and dissolved into tears. This isn't how the Olympic Games were supposed to be. I simply couldn't go on. I had nothing left to give. I couldn't handle any more pain or disappointment. I just wanted to get out of there.

Apparently Coach had figured that this moment would come. When he saw that I had no more strength, he stepped in to be that strength. With deep compassion and loving firmness, he told me that the most important thing now was for me to finish this meet, and let God take care of the rest. We hadn't gone through eight events to stop now.

"Dave, I don't know what the pain feels like," he said. "I know that the emotional pain and everything else has got to be hard for you. But I'm your coach, and I'm saying that we can finish this."

"I don't think so," I complained.

"Well—I *do* think so." As he spoke, I could see the tears in his own eyes. He loved me and cared about me like a father. But even more, he believed in me and in God's greater purpose for my life. He put his arms around me and for a few minutes we cried together.

At this point I had to have some kind of painkiller if I was going to finish. So Coach brought in one of the doctors to evaluate my foot and give me an injection. He inserted the needle down through the top of my foot, hoping to deaden the area around the navicular bone. The shots could have been administered earlier, but it's so hard to predict their effect on performance that both Franson and I had wanted to avoid them unless absolutely necessary.

I understood why when I went out to throw the javelin. The shot did nothing for the pain, and only made my foot harder to control. I lost my footing and nearly fell on the first throw, which landed far short. At least it pleased the partisan crowd. For the second attempt, I played it safe by taking six or seven steps before throwing instead of my usual runup. Although it was nowhere near my best, the toss went far enough to lift me from sixth place into third—making me a silver or bronze medal contender. Unfortunately, before I had a chance to take my last throw, another error by the officials caused my time to elapse, resulting in a foul. To do so poorly in my best event and then be denied a final throw only served to extinguish the last tiny flame of desire to go on. I didn't care about the bronze or the silver medal; I wasn't going to finish anyway.

As I stumbled through the javelin competition, Coach Franson watched and cheered me on from a nearby section of the stands. A little American boy, probably ten or eleven years old, saw him yelling to me, and came up alongside him.

"Is that Dave?" the boy said.

"Yeah." Coach was pretty upset himself, and didn't really feel like talking.

"Dave's gonna win, huh?" said the boy.

"No, I don't think so."

"How come? Isn't he from the Dan and Dave commercials?"

"Yeah, but he's got a broken foot. He broke it just before coming here."

The boy's eyes widened. "Really? Then what's he doing out there? How can he do that stuff on a broken foot?"

"Because he wants to do his very best. He's an American, and this is the Olympics. He's not going to give up."

The boy stood there for a minute, as if to take in the significance of Coach's words. Finally he said, "Well, tell Dave to hang in there and give it everything he's got, OK?"

Then a thought occurred to Coach. "You know why Dave's still out there?" he said. "Because of little guys just like you. As you get older, you're gonna have times when you want to give up and quit, and that's when you can think of Dave. Remember, don't ever give up, just like Dave isn't giving up. Even though he's not going to win, he's gonna finish because of kids like you." His words seemed to hit home for the boy, who left feeling pretty psyched up.

Down on the field, I wanted to give up and quit.

After the javelin disaster, I told the doctors that the shot didn't help. My foot was spasming and shutting down. Coach and Kevin joined me as they decided to give one more injection. This time, while I lay on the examining table, they stuck the needle straight up through my arch. Words can't begin to describe the pain I felt as he moved the needle around to apply medication in different areas. It hurt more than the stress fracture itself, and I couldn't control my tears. Everything came rushing out at once—the agony, the anger, the fear, the despair. It seemed to me that if someone had to drive a huge needle into my foot, it was time to throw in the towel. I asked Franson if I should quit. I asked Kevin if I should quit. I asked God if I should quit.

"Dave," Coach said, "I think this whole thing is way bigger than you and I even realize. I just finished talking with a boy who thinks you're the greatest thing in the world because you're out there competing on a broken foot." He went on to tell me about his conversation.

"You've got to believe, Dave, that God is allowing an incredible story to unfold through this Olympic Games. It's not the story we thought it would be, and it may not have the same audience you'd have if you'd won the gold medal, with all its glamor and glory. It's really a deep and broad story about lots and lots of people who've stood behind you. It's about a dream, a disappointment, and then about not giving up. You know the Olympics is not really about winning gold medals; it's about that phrase in the Olympic creed: 'Not to have conquered, but to have fought well.'"

We all cried some more. Maybe Coach was right. Maybe something bigger was going on that I didn't understand. Maybe God wanted me to learn that greatness was not so much about being the best, but about *striving* to be the best, not so much about winning as about enduring.

I began to picture the image of Christ again, and the pain he went through. He, too, was stabbed in the foot as they nailed him to that cross. But he was dying for me and for all of humanity. As bad as my pain was, it paled in comparison to his.

Coach, Kevin, and I prayed together for strength to make it through the 1500 meters—one metric mile. I stepped down from the table, but I couldn't tell my foot had hit the floor. The bottom was completely numb. And as I tried to jog on it, I still felt pain. It was hopeless. How could I run safely if I couldn't feel the ground under me? I'd land on it incorrectly and completely break off my foot, like racehorses sometimes do.

"I can't go out there," I said, "I'll be an embarrassment to my country."

"Embarrassment?" Coach said. "That would be the *last* thing anyone would say about you. You're going out and overcoming the odds. It's hard enough for an athlete to get here at all, and you've not only gotten here, but you might actually

win a bronze medal in spite of this injury. You've already performed this decathlon at a world-class level on a broken foot.
Dave, you've *got* to run. You've got to finish this."

"OK, I'll run," I said at last. "But I have no idea what's
going to happen. After a hundred meters I could go down."

"Then go down," Coach said, "but then get up again and
walk if you have to."

Pulling myself together, I determined to make it through
this last event. I walked out on the track still trying to act like
nothing was wrong with my foot—why, I don't know. My
group lined up under the stadium lights at about 10 p.m. At
the gun, I almost fell, but caught myself and managed to establish a rhythm, though my right foot dragged. I had to look
down every now and then to see if it was landing properly. It
felt so strange—numb on the bottom, painful on the top. I figured I'd just stop if it hurt too much.

As I ran, several other things were going on. Coach had
been invited up into the NBC Triplecast booth to offer commentary on the race. He explained to the world what had happened to my foot, and that even though my dream of a gold
medal was out of reach, I had chosen to give it my best anyway.
The network had also put a mike and a camera on Mom and
Dad during the last two events so people could hear their com-
ments and reactions.

After the first lap I thought, *OK, I can stop now—I gave it a
try.* But something in me said to keep going. The crowd was
screaming—mostly for their own decathletes, but it gave me
extra energy.

At 800 meters, I said, *You're halfway there now—you might
as well keep running.* Finishing was now a realistic goal. I
thought about medals—the one I'd probably get, and the one I
really wanted. But at this point medals no longer mattered. I
knew I'd achieved something much more important.

Adrenaline must have kicked in for the rest of the race,
because the pain in my foot diminished. I was actually able to
pick up speed at the end.

We all knew who the three medalists were at the finish
line. Robert Zmelik of Czechoslovakia took the gold, Antonio

Penalver of Spain the silver, and I had the bronze. After a congratulatory hug, the three of us clasped hands and raised our arms for the photographers. Then they took off for their victory lap. I would have run with them, but my foot had completely shut down and I could hardly walk. With a large icebag around my ankle and an American flag wrapped around me, I hobbled around the track, stopping to hug my parents and Sheri.

It was over. I had run the race before me. I had finished. I had won the bronze medal. It had been a long journey from Missoula to Barcelona, but thanks to constant encouragement of Coach Franson, Coach Bakley, Kevin, Sheri, my parents, my friends, and especially the Lord, I had survived.

1500 meters

PR: 4:23.00

It's finally here, the event you've been dreading for the past two days—no, the past two *weeks*. When I finish the pole vault and start to look ahead to the 1500 meters, my reaction is always the same: *How did I get myself into this again? I've been here before. I didn't want to be here then, and I don't want to be here now.*

My body—and that of most decathletes—is clearly not made for this event. I probably weigh seventy-five pounds more than the guys who run the open 1500 meters. If I were to race them, they'd lap me several times. You can at least *imagine* yourself as Carl Lewis in the 100 meters or the long jump, or Jackie Joyner-Kersee in the heptathlon, or Roger Kingdom in the hurdles. But when you step into the 1500 meters, there's no one you can even remotely compare yourself to. You feel as if you're showing the whole world what a slowpoke you are. Even so, it requires an incredible amount of effort, endurance, and courage.

The main question I always ask myself before I run the 1500 is, *Do I merely want to finish, or do I want to finish well?* After all, I've been torturing myself for the past two days, and it seems unfair for the final event to be a gut-splitting mile-long race. But after years of training, and fifteen or twenty decathlons, you no longer wonder *whether* you can do it. The only question is *how well* you'll do it. That's where the real courage comes in. Do you have what it takes to run harder and faster than you've ever run before?

With the 1500, you know ahead of time exactly how your performance will translate into a final score for the whole decathlon. Your coach has checked the point scale and informed you that a time of 4:20, for instance, will be worth so many points and will give you a total score of so much. Then you must decide whether you're willing to invest the energy to reach that time. You can settle for less than you're capable of, or you can give every last ounce and bring out the most from yourself.

Just before the race, it's not uncommon for the decathletes to talk among themselves about what time they'll probably run. "I'm going for a 4:30, but most likely I'll run a 4:35," someone might say. It may sound funny to share information with the competition, but in the decathlon your main competition is yourself. Both you and the competition will actually perform better by comparing notes. Why? If you and someone else are both shooting for about the same time, you can run together and help each other stay on pace.

And there's one other minor detail I forgot to mention: Running the 1500 will hurt like the dickens. You're using up the remainder of two stores of energy—the last one-tenth of your total energy for the decathlon, and then the last bit of that one-tenth for the end of this race. When you finish, your energy reserve should be exactly at zero. You'll feel pain no matter how slow you run, but if you resolve to give a full one hundred percent, you'll hurt a lot more. The payoff will be a better time and a higher score.

The 1500 has taught me the value of pursuing excellence from start to finish rather than slacking off or settling for mediocrity when the end is in sight. The temptation to "just get by" is real—both in the 1500 and in life—but the more often we give in to it, the easier it is for us to make it a habit.

I've also learned that human beings have an incredibly deep well of inner strength to draw from. We've all had experiences—crises, deadlines, challenges—where we were required to keep giving of ourselves when we didn't think we had anything left to give. But somehow we managed to muster the emotional strength to get through the situation successfully. The well we thought was dry actually had a reserve of cool, fresh water. I think God made us that way. And I believe it's possible for all of us to tap that well of energy, whether we're running the 1500 meters or the race of life.

▪ Epilogue ▪

THERE'S A PHRASE I heard in a Whitney Houston song a few years ago that intrigued me: "My finest day is yet unknown." I can't say what the songwriter meant by those words, but they really clicked for me as a helpful way to view my life and my goals.

For years I've been aiming for what many see as an ultimate life goal—winning the Olympic gold medal in the decathlon. I always figured that when I did win, that would be my finest day.

But the more I thought about that view, something didn't seem quite right. After I reach that goal and win the Games, then what? If that is my finest day, is there nothing more to look forward to? Or suppose I don't reach that goal. Does that mean my finest day has passed me by? No.

I haven't lived my whole life just for the Olympics. There's so much more to life than that. Obviously, I've devoted more than a decade to winning a gold medal, so it's very important to me. But I know it's only one part of the total picture of my life. I want to keep reaching higher for other goals and dreams after my Olympic years end.

That's where the song comes in. As far as the decathlon, I've reached many of the goals I've set for myself, and it feels great. But to know that there are always more goals for me to reach makes life exciting. I will never "arrive" in this life; I'm always on the way to something better. In other words, "my finest day is yet unknown."

Actually, for me and for all Christians, my finest day *is* known, though it won't take place on earth. My finest day will be the day I show up in heaven, when I'll be able to have my picture taken with my arm around Jesus Christ. That will be one incredible day. And guess what—I won't be able to bring my bronze medal with me — or the gold when I win it. All I'll bring is the person Christ made me into while I was here on earth.

I ended up learning much more about life by not winning the gold. Don't get me wrong— I'm still disappointed I didn't win, and I still struggle at times with anger at God for the way it happened. But the message from him continues to come through that his loving purpose is being worked out in my life.

If I'd won the gold, I might be saying something different when I speak at schools, churches, and businesses around the country. I might be saying, "Hey, it's great at the top—and maybe if you try hard enough, you can be just like me. Then you can sit back and enjoy fame and fortune."

Instead, I'm able to say something much more real, and ultimately more hopeful. Yes, we should set our sights high and go for our goals and dreams with all our heart—just as I am still going for mine. We should believe in the talents God has given us and strive to give nothing less than one hundred percent of ourselves. We should hang in there when the going gets tough. I tell kids to get out and "kick major booty."

But in the final analysis, reaching the goal or realizing the dream is not nearly as important as the person we've become along the way. Long after the thrill of victory or the agony of defeat has faded, that person will endure. The more we allow ourselves to learn and grow in the *process* of reaching our goals, the better equipped we'll be to live a meaningful life and make a difference in the world.

After the Barcelona Games had ended, both Sheri and I were sick of the Olympics and sick of the decathlon. But on the plane back to New York, where we were to appear on *The Maury Povich Show* before going home, the members of the organizing committee for the Atlanta Games in 1996 sat a few seats in front of us. Their enthusiasm was so contagious that by the time our plane landed, I knew I wanted to go.

Surgeons later repaired the bone in my foot with a couple of screws, and I decided not to compete in 1993 to allow it to heal completely. It turned out to be an extremely busy year for me, with many speaking engagements. Apparently people did want to hear the story of a guy who gutted it out even though he knew he wasn't going to win. And speaking to them gave me the opportunity to give something back to the Christian community, the Olympic community, and others who had made such a difference in my own life.

Athletically, I've gotten to do some fun things since Barcelona. I've participated in a number of golf tournaments, including ones sponsored by Michael Jordan and Magic Johnson. And for the past two years I've competed in—and won—the annual Jeep Superstars competition in which celebrity athletes from all different sports battle it out in areas that are not their specialty, such as kayaking, swimming, cycling, and running obstacle courses.

But the most profound change in my life since the Barcelona Games occurred last year when Sheri and I adopted a beautiful daughter, Alexandra, who has brought a whole new meaning to life for us. Sheri has been thrilled to have her own child to love and care for, and I've enjoyed my new role as father.

Now I'm back to full-time training and competing again. My sights are set for the '96 Olympic Games. Barring injury or some other unforseen circumstance, I intend to be there, healthy and hungry for the gold medal.

"Who is the world's greatest athlete—Dan or Dave? To be settled in Atlanta." Hmm—I like the sound of that.

BRONZE . . . BUT GOLD

A tribute to a great Christian warrior: Dave Johnson

God's warrior stands . . . surveys the field.
Intense, courageous, Christlike, bold.
Injury and pain have now revealed
The challenge great to win the gold.

A friend gone down . . . the tension builds.
Alone the eagle's torch to hold.
"The task ahead will press my skills . . .
I'll give my best to go for gold."

His eyes were fixed upon the One
Whose life and death had changed his soul.
"I must in throw and jump and run
Give Him the glory in quest for gold."

"For what I am and have are His . . .
He is my King . . . I can't withhold
In witnessing for win or miss . . .
He must be first before the gold."

Though suffering, hurt, no excuse was heard.
Ten grueling events had taken toll.
On medal stand not first . . . but third.
To human eyes . . . the bronze, not gold.

With focused spirit beyond all measure,
He gave thousands, young and old,
A performance bequeathed to memory's treasure
Although he could not wear the gold.

A head held high . . . he'd given his best.
This athlete's sermon must oft be told
To those who follow in Olympic test
To know the worth of bronze and gold.

For human honor always given
With trophy destined to rust and mold,
This victory won applause from heaven:
"My son! My son! . . . YES, BRONZE . . . BUT GOLD!"

Oft asked to whom he give the prize . . .
The millions hear and lives unfold
To catch the vision of Kingdom eyes.
"We see the mettle . . . YES, BRONZE . . . BUT GOLD."

—Dr. Don O. Berryhill
August 20, 1992

Photosection credits:

Page One

Victah Sailer, Agence Shot

Page Two

Johnson family collection

Page Three

Background and A: Johnson family collection
Inset, upper right: Photo by Lawrence Photography

Page Four

Johnson family collection

Page Five

Johnson family collection

Page Six

Sheri Johnson

Page Seven

Sheri Johnson

Page Nine

Background and inset, upper right: Sheri Johnson

Page Ten

A and B: Sheri Johnson
Background: Johnson family collection

Page Eleven

Sheri Johnson

Page Twelve

Background: Sheri Johnson
A: Allsport Photography; Mike Powell, photographer
B: Johnson family collection

Page Thirteen

Sheri Johnson

Page Fourteen

1. Victah Sailer, Agence Shot
2. Victah Sailer, Agence Shot
3. Victah Sailer, Agence Shot
4. Allsport Photography; Mike Powell, photographer
5. Focus On Sports Inc.
6. Focus On Sports Inc.
7. Allsport Photography; Mike Powell, photographer
8. Victah Sailer, Agence Shot
9. Victah Sailer, Agence Shot
10. Sheri Johnson